FORAGING OREGON

Help Us Keep This Guide Up to Date

Every effort has been made by the author and editors to make this guide as accurate and useful as possible. However, many things can change after a guide is published.

We would appreciate hearing from you concerning your experiences with this guide and how you feel it could be improved and kept up to date. While we may not be able to respond to all comments and suggestions, we'll take them to heart, and we'll also make certain to share them with the author. Please send your comments and suggestions to the following email address: falconeditorial@rowman.com

Thanks for your input, and happy foraging!

FORAGING OREGON

Finding, Identifying, and Preparing
Edible Wild Foods in Oregon

Second Edition

Christopher Nyerges

ESSEX, CONNECTICUT

FALCONGUIDES®

An imprint of Globe Pequot, the trade division of
The Rowman & Littlefield Publishing Group, Inc.
4501 Forbes Blvd., Ste. 200
Lanham, MD 20706
www.rowman.com

Falcon and FalconGuides are registered trademarks and Make Adventure Your Story is a trademark of
The Rowman & Littlefield Publishing Group, Inc.

Distributed by NATIONAL BOOK NETWORK

Photos by Christopher Nyerges unless otherwise noted
Maps by Melissa Baker and The Rowman & Littlefield Publishing Group, Inc.

British Library Cataloguing in Publication Information available

Library of Congress Cataloging-in-Publication Data

ISBN 978-1-4930-6445-8 (paper: alk. paper)
ISBN 978-1-4930-6446-5 (electronic)

∞™ The paper used in this publication meets the minimum requirements of American National Standard for Information Sciences—Permanence of Paper for Printed Library Materials, ANSI/NISO Z39.48-1992.

The author and The Rowman & Littlefield Publishing Group, Inc., assume no liability for accidents happening to, or injuries sustained by, readers who engage in the activities described in this book.

CONTENTS

Foreword xi
Acknowledgments xiv
Introduction 1
   Scope of This Book 1
   Organization 2
Plants Listed by Environment Type 3
Collecting and Harvesting Wild Foods 7
How Much Wild Food Is Out There, Anyway? 9
Are Wild Foods Nutritious?. 11

SEAWEEDS. 14
Marine Green Algae (Chlorophyta); Brown Algae (Phaeophyta);
Red Algae (Rhodophyta) 15

FERNS. 18
Bracken Family (Dennstaedtiacea) 19
   Bracken (*Pteridium aquilinum*) 19

GYMNOSPERMS 22
Pine Family (Pinaceae) 23
   Pine (*Pinus* spp.) 23

MAGNOLIIDS 25
Laurel Family (Lauraceae). 26
   Oregon Myrtle (*Umbellularia californica*) 26

EUDICOTS 29
Muskroot Family (Adoxaceae) 30
   Elderberry (*Sambucus* spp.) 30
Amaranth Family (Amaranthaceae) 34
   Amaranth (*Amaranthus* spp.). 34
Carrot (or Parsley) Family (Apiaceae) 37
   Wild Carrot (*Daucus carota*) 37
   Fennel (*Foeniculum vulgare*) 40
   Cow Parsnip (*Heracleum maximum,* formerly *H. lanatum*). 42

Sunflower Family (Asteraceae) 44
    GROUP 4
    Burdock (*Arctium minus* and *A. lappa*). 44
    Thistle (*Cirsium* spp.) 47
    GROUP 5
    Pineapple Weed (*Matricaria discoidea,* formerly *M. matricarioides*). 49
    GROUP 7
    Chicory (*Cichorium intybus*) 51
    Cat's Ear (*Hypochaeris radicata*) 54
    Prickly Lettuce (*Lactuca serriola*, et al.). 56
    Nipplewort (*Lapsana communis*) 59
    Sow Thistle (*Sonchus oleraceus*, et al.). 61
    Dandelion (*Taraxacum officinale*). 64
Barberry Family (Berberidaceae) 67
    Oregon Grape (*Mahonia aquifolium*) 67
Birch Family (Betulaceae). 70
    Hazelnut (*Corylus cornuta*). 70
Borage (or Waterleaf) Family (Boraginaceae) 72
    Mountain Bluebells (*Mertensia ciliata*) 72
Mustard Family (Brassicaceae) 74
    Wintercress (*Barbarea vulgaris* and *B. verna*). 74
    Mustard (*Brassica* spp.). 77
    Sea Rocket (*Cakile edentula* and *C. maritima*) 81
    Bittercress (*Cardamine* spp.) 84
    Shepherd's Purse (*Capsella bursa-pastoris*). 86
    Watercress (*Nasturtium officinale*) 88
    Wild Radish (*Raphanus sativus* and *R. raphanistrum*). 92
    Hedge Mustard (*Sisymbrium* spp.) 96
Cactus Family (Cactaceae) 99
    Prickly Pear (*Opuntia* spp.). 99
Pink Family (Caryophyllaceae) 103
    Chickweed (*Stellaria media*) 103
Goosefoot Family (Chenopodiaceae) 107
    Orach (*Atriplex hastata*) 107
    Lamb's Quarter, White and Green (*Chenopodium album* and *C. murale*). . . 110
    Glasswort, aka Pickleweed (*Salicornia* spp.) 113
Heath Family (Ericaceae) 116
    Madrone (*Arbutus menziesii*). 116
    Manzanita (*Arctostaphylos* spp.). 120
    Salal (*Gaultheria shallon*) 123
    Huckleberry and Blueberry (*Vaccinium* spp.). 126

Oak Family (Fagaceae) 130
    Oak Tree (*Quercus* spp.) 130
Geranium Family (Geraniaceae) 134
    Filaree (*Erodium* spp.) 134
Gooseberry Family (Grossulariaceae) 137
    Currants and Gooseberries (*Ribes* spp.). 137
Mint Family (Lamiaceae) 141
    Mint (*Mentha* spp.) 141
Mallow Family (Malvaceae). 144
    Mallow (*Malva neglecta*) 144
Miner's Lettuce Family (Montiaceae) 147
    Spring Beauty (*Claytonia lanceolata*) 147
    Miner's Lettuce (*Claytonia perfoliata*) 149
Evening Primrose Family (Onagraceae). 152
    Fireweed (*Chamerion angustifolium*) 152
Oxalis Family (Oxalidaceae) 156
    Sour Grass, aka Wood Sorrel (*Oxalis* spp.) 156
Lopseed Family (Phrymaceae) 158
    Yellow Monkey Flower (*Mimulus guttatus*) 158
Plantain Family (Plantaginaceae) 160
    Plantain (*Plantago major* and *P. lanceolata*) 160
    Veronica, aka Speedwell (*Veronica americana*) 163
Buckwheat Family (Polygonaceae) 165
    American Bistort (*Bistorta bistortoides*) 165
    Mountain Sorrel (*Oxyria dignya*). 168
    Sheep Sorrel (*Rumex acetosella*). 170
    Curly Dock (*Rumex crispus*) and Broad-Leafed Dock (*Rumex obtusifolius*) . . 172
Purslane Family (Portulacaceae). 176
    Purslane (*Portulaca oleraceae*). 176
Rose Family (Rosaceae) 179
    Serviceberry, aka Juneberry (*Amelanchier alnifolia*) . . . 179
    Strawberry (*Fragaria* spp.) 181
    Indian Plum (*Oemleria cerasiformis*) 184
    Wild Cherries (*Prunus* spp.) 187
    Wild Rose (*Rosa* spp.) 190
    Blackberry (*Rubus* spp.) 192
Nightshade Family (Solanaceae) 196
    Black Nightshade (*Solanum nigrum*) 196
Nettle Family (Urticaceae) 199
    Stinging Nettle (*Urtica dioica*) 199

Violet Family (Violaceae) 203
    Violet (*Viola* spp.) 203

MONOCOTS **205**
Onion (or Garlic) Family (Alliaceae) 206
    Wild Onions, et al. (*Allium* spp.) 206
Rush Family (Juncaceae) 209
    Rush (*Juncus textilis*, et al.) 209
Asparagus Family (Asparagaceae) 213
    Wild Asparagus (*Asparagus officinalis*) 213
    Camas (*Camassia quamash*) 217
    Death Camas (*Zigadenus elegans* and *Z. venenosus*) 220
Grass Family (Poaceae) 221
Cattail Family (Typhaceae) 224
    Cattail (*Typha* spp.) 224

Other Edibles 228
Getting Started 230
Test Your Knowledge of Plants 233
The Dozen Easiest-to-Recognize, Most Widespread, Most Versatile
    Wild Foods of Oregon 237
Staff of Life: Best Wild-Food Bread Sources 239
Sweet Tooth: Best Wild-Food Sugars and Desserts 242
Learn the Families 245
Useful References 255
Index 257
About the Author 261

FOREWORD

Christopher Nyerges is the real thing. He has been teaching, lecturing, and leading field trips related to survival skills for over forty years through his School of Self-Reliance. The book goes beyond most of its kind in the enthusiasm about and personal experimentation and use of the plants the author includes. His firsthand experiences and insights into preparation and notes on palatability of edible plants from urban to wilderness environments add immensely to the usefulness of the book. Through his writing, Nyerges encourages us to seek food independence and attain a higher level of self-sufficiency and better health through the use of the edible plants around us.

Foraging Oregon should prove useful to backpackers, hikers, the lost and hungry, survivalists, and adventurous food explorers in Oregon and neighboring areas. In this, his twenty-second book, Nyerges provides a detailed compendium of over one hundred edible native and introduced plants available throughout the seasons in Oregon's diverse ecosystems, including urban areas. He pulls together the data from written works, interviews, and his own extensive personal research. The following quote is a testimony to Nyerges's dedication:

> *To give some examples of the many ways in which we can eat miner's lettuce, consider a weekend survival trip I once led for a dozen young men. Our only food was what we fished or foraged, and there was very little growing in the area besides miner's lettuce. We had miner's lettuce salad, miner's lettuce soup, fried miner's lettuce, boiled miner's lettuce, miner's lettuce cooked with fish, and miner's lettuce broth! If we were in a kitchen with all sorts of condiments, we'd have had miner's lettuce omelettes, and soufflés, and stir-fries, and green drinks.*

In the text, after treating the seaweeds, bracken ferns, and pines, Nyerges moves on to *Umbellularia* (Oregon myrtle; now segregated from mainstream flowering plants). The remaining plant profiles are first divided into the two great flowering plant groups, the eudicots (formerly dicots) and the monocots, then alphabetically into thirty-four families, according to the latest botanical classifications. The selection of edible plants for this book is based on his perspective of "the plants that a person attempting to live off the land would actually be eating." A robust index to scientific and common names makes all entries easily accessible to the botanically inclined as well as to the botanical novice.

While this botanical family approach may put off some, there is a very good reason for organizing the entries this way. As noted periodically in the text, Nyerges was influenced heavily by his early ethnobotanical studies with Dr. Leonid Enari, senior biologist for many years at the Los Angeles County Arboretum

Dr. James Bauml, botanist

& Botanic Garden, who was a teacher and mentor to the author. (I knew and respected Dr. Enari, my predecessor at the arboretum, for his commitment to sharing his knowledge with the public in his classes Edible, Medicinal, and Poisonous Plants and Plant Taxonomy.) Dr. Enari's teachings and encouragement inspired Nyerges to dedicate this book to his former teacher. Dr. Enari pointed out to his students the plant families and genera that were entirely safe to eat (albeit not all of them tasty or tender), a valuable insight and shortcut for any student once they have learned a family's salient features, and these teachings come through clearly in the book.

Each entry's narrative is preceded by a synopsis containing Use, Range, Similarity to toxic species, Best time (to collect), Status, Tools needed, and Properties. Range refers to several general ecosystems among the diverse life zones in Oregon where that particular plant is most likely to be found: desert, ocean, foothills, mountains, alpine, riparian, and urban and fields. The volume includes many helpful recipes for preparing the wild foods. Photographs by the author, his friends, and his wife help immensely with identifications and bring form to the descriptions.

Nyerges honors the memory of Native American knowledge, and he often relates Indian traditional food uses, harvesting, and preparation of plants he is discussing. Another interesting dimension to the book is his citing edible plant references from the field notes of Lewis and Clark as they crossed Oregon on their celebrated journey. Seven charts summarize supplemental information: wild food nutritional composition; acorn chemical composition; traditional diets with complementary grains and legumes; the dozen best (easy-to-recognize, widespread, versatile) wild food plants; best wild foods for breads; and best wild sugars and desserts.

Reading this book, one is reminded of the biblical passage Matthew 6:26 from the Sermon on the Mount. From the King James Version, the passage is as follows:

> *Behold the fowls of the air: for they sow not, neither do they reap, nor gather into barns; yet your heavenly Father feedeth them. Are ye not much better than they?*

Indeed, this book will bolster your faith in the knowledge that you will find food if you carry it with you. It will help readers believe in the abundance of wild foods within reach in all corners of Oregon, and wherever else these same plants are found.

After reading this book you will be aware that there are fewer "weeds" and more edible and healthful plants all around you. With this book you can reawaken the consciousness of your forebearers who hunted and gathered all that they consumed. You can eat fresh, local, more healthfully, and for less money with the insights in *Foraging Oregon*.

—Dr. James Bauml, botanist

ACKNOWLEDGMENTS

After I had already begun my lifelong study of botany and ethnobotany in high school and college, I had the very good fortune in approximately 1974 to meet Dr. Leonid Enari. Dr. Enari was the senior biologist at the Los Angeles County Arboretum and taught his course on edible, medicinal, and poisonous plants as well as taxonomy. His knowledge was astronomical.

After I took several of his courses, he allowed me to come to his office for private consultations, where he would identify the various plants I brought him and tell me their stories. Never once did I bring him a plant that he didn't know. He eagerly worked with me on my first book (*Guide to Wild Foods*, published in 1978), assisting me with fine details such as the Latin terms. He also worked with me to compile an appendix of safe and primarily edible plant families, which he considered the only legitimate "shortcut" way to study wild foods.

Dr. Enari's unique background in botany and chemistry made him ideally suited as a primary source of information. He earned two higher degrees in both botany and chemistry (equivalent of PhD) in his 20s before emigrating to the United States from Estonia, where he experienced some of the results of Nazi occupation. He would tell his students that he pursued these fields because he desired to help people. "With the knowledge of botany and chemistry," he once told the class, "no one need ever go hungry."

When he first moved to the United States, he settled in Portland, Oregon, and taught at Lewis and Clark College and the University of Portland. He eventually moved to Southern California. While living in the Northwest, Dr. Enari researched and wrote *Plants of the Pacific Northwest*, the result of about forty field trips. I have used that book as one of my primary references.

Dr. Enari acted as my teacher, mentor, and friend, and he always encouraged me on to further research as well as teaching and writing. I felt the great loss when he passed away in 2006 at age 89.

To Dr. Enari, I dedicate this book on Oregon wild foods.

I also had many other mentors, teachers, and supporters along the way. These include (but are not limited to) Dr. Luis Wheeler (USC botanist), Richard Barmakian (nutritionist), Dorothy Poole (Gabrielino "chaparral granny"), Richard E. White (founder of WTI, who taught me how to teach, and how to think), John Watkins (a Mensan who "knew everything"), and Mr. Muir (my botany teacher at John Muir High School). These individuals all imparted some important aspect to me, and they have all been my mentors to varying degrees. I thank them for their influence. Euell Gibbons also had a strong influence on my early studies of wild food, mostly through his books; I met him only once.

Over twenty years ago, I met John Kallas, who I regard as the top wild-food man of Oregon and the Pacific Northwest. Kallas's field trips, workshops, and books are strongly recommended for anyone living in Oregon and the surrounding area. With a doctorate in botany, he is a remarkable resource for Oregon and the Northwest. I want to thank Dr. Kallas for his assistance with this book.

Of course, there have been many others who taught me bits and pieces along the way, and I feel gratitude for everyone whose love of the multifaceted art of ethnobotany has touched me in some way. Some of these friends and strong supporters have included Pascal Baudar and Mia Wasilevich, Peter Gail, Gary Gonzales, Dude McLean, Alan Halcon, Paul Campbell, Rick and Karen Adams, Barbara Kolander, Jim Robertson, Timothy Snider, and Dr. Norman Wakeman.

Special thanks to Dr. James Bauml, who assisted with the preparation of this manuscript and who wrote the foreword.

I also want to extend a special thanks to my beloved wife, Helen, for her support of this project.

Photo Credits

Yes, I took many of the photos in this book, but I couldn't do it all myself. Rick Adams deserves special thanks for the many trips we took together to get photos. My dear Helen also provided many photos, as did my dear stepdaughter Barbara Kolander. Other folks who contributed photos include Arthur Aaron, Zoya Akulova, Angie Au, Dan Baird, Ron and Anthony Baniaga, Matt Below, Barry Breckling, Kyle Chamberlain, Christie, Debra Cook, John Doyen, Tim Hagan, Louis-M. Landry, Jeff Martin, Steve Matson, Keir Morse, J. K. Nelson, Jean Pawek, Aaron Schusteff, Bob Sivinski, Vernon Smith, Robert Steers, Bob Sweatt, Simon Tonge, Dr. Amadej Trnkoczy, and Lily Jane Tsong. I thank you all!

INTRODUCTION

We owe a debt of gratitude to the generations of indigenous peoples of North America whose lives and livelihood depended on plants for food and everything else. Much of this knowledge has been passed down generation to generation, and much has been rediscovered by researchers.

Many of the living "old ways" have been lost, but the knowledge of how to utilize the plants of the land has not been entirely forgotten. Various generations have realized the great value of knowing how to identify and use what nature has provided, even though this information waxes and wanes in importance in the general viewpoint.

When there is war or depression or famine, we desire to rekindle this link to our past and hope for our future. When times are good, and money flows, we forget our roots. Just fifty years ago, you were considered poor, to be pitied, if you actually used wild foods.

With Euell Gibbons in the early 1970s, the tide began to turn again, and today everyone wants to know at least a little about our national heritage of wild foods. Everyone wants to be self-sufficient and be a part of the solution. And today we have an abundance of books, videos, and classes to teach us about these skills.

In addition to the native flora, we now have an abundance of introduced plants and common edible weeds, which were used for generations throughout Europe and Asia. Sometimes these introduced flora are a blessing, sometimes not.

Scope of This Book

Foraging Oregon covers plants that can be used primarily for food and are common in Oregon. We are not attempting to cover every single edible plant that could possibly be used for food, or those that are very marginal as food. Our focus is on those wild foods that are widespread, easily recognizable and identifiable, and sufficient to *create* meals. Many of the wild edibles that are too localized or only provide a marginal source of food are not included. Plants that are endangered or have the possibility of being endangered have not been included. In general, plants that are too easily confused with something poisonous have also been omitted.

The content of this book is intended to be useful for hikers and backpackers, and for anyone in urban areas where so many of these plants still grow. Our goal is to provide a book that details the plants that a person attempting to live off the land would actually be eating. Our goal was not to provide a complete list of every possible plant in Oregon that could be eaten if there was nothing else to eat. But believe me, if you embark on the study of ethnobotany and start working closely with a mentor/teacher, your learning will expand way beyond the pages of this book, and that is how it should be.

This is not a book about medicinal properties, and though some medicinal aspects will be addressed in passing, we will provide some ideal references in the back of the book. Nor does this book focus on exclusively native plants. If you're hungry in the woods, or in your own backyard, you don't care if the plant is native or introduced, right?

Organization

The plants in this book are organized according to the system used by botanists.

Many books on plants organize the plants by flower color or environmental niche, both of which have their adherents and their pitfalls. However, this book categorizes the plants according to their families, which gives you a broader perspective on many more plants than can be reasonably put into one book. As you will see, many of the genera (and some families) are entirely safe to use as food. This is how I was taught by my teacher and mentor, Dr. Leonid Enari, since he believed that—though there is no shortcut to learning about the identity and uses of plants—understanding the families will impart a far greater insight into the scope of "wild foods."

We'll start with the seaweeds, ferns, and then the gymnosperms (the cone-bearing plants). Then, we'll work our way through the flowering plants, in alphabetical order by their Latin family names, first the dicots, then the monocots.

PLANTS LISTED BY ENVIRONMENT TYPE

In our selection of plants for *Foraging Oregon*, we've attempted to include common edible plants from the different environments of the state. Below, you will see the basic categories of desert, ocean, foothills, mountains, alpine, riparian, and urban and fields. But keep in mind that there is often a lot of overlap from one ecosystem to another. Some introduced exotics, for example, can be found just about everywhere. On the other hand, seaweed and glasswort will only be found in the ocean environment.

As a handy reference to the plants in this book, note the biological zone where each plant is *most likely* to be encountered. Some plants are only found in one zone, but others can be found in several of these zones.

Oregon is a unique place with several intersecting ecological and cultural zones. Just look at a map of the state. During a conversation with a woman from the Oregon Native Plant Society, she told me that when most outsiders think of Oregon, they only think of the western third—the green forest of the Cascades all the way down the slopes to the ocean. And yes, that is part of the rich landscape of Oregon. The Native peoples of the Northwest Coast region lived in a land of abundance and wealth. Tribes who lived in this area had all the riches of the ocean, like salmon and mussels and seals. And the mountains of the Northwest Coast also provided deer, elk, and other hunting opportunities, as well as the rich flora of the coast and mountains.

And yet, the eastern part of the state is really a high desert.

The Great Basin—which encompasses most of Nevada—extends into the southeastern part of Oregon into the Harney Basin. This large area has the Sierra Nevada range to the west and the Rocky Mountains in the east. This was a tough place to live off the land, and the Native people who lived here practiced hunting and gathering and some agriculture. They used cattails and ate berries, pine nuts, and various edible roots.

The Columbia Plateau encompasses most of the eastern part of Oregon. It's a highland area bordered by the Cascades in the west and the Rocky Mountains in the east. Culturally, the plateau area was considered a transitional zone, with the Columbia River and the Fraser River systems being integral to trade.

Each of these areas is rich in its own history of the Native Americans who were here for thousands of years. There is also the history of the Lewis and Clark expedition (with the many ethnobotanical details that were recorded), which passed through Oregon's northern border.

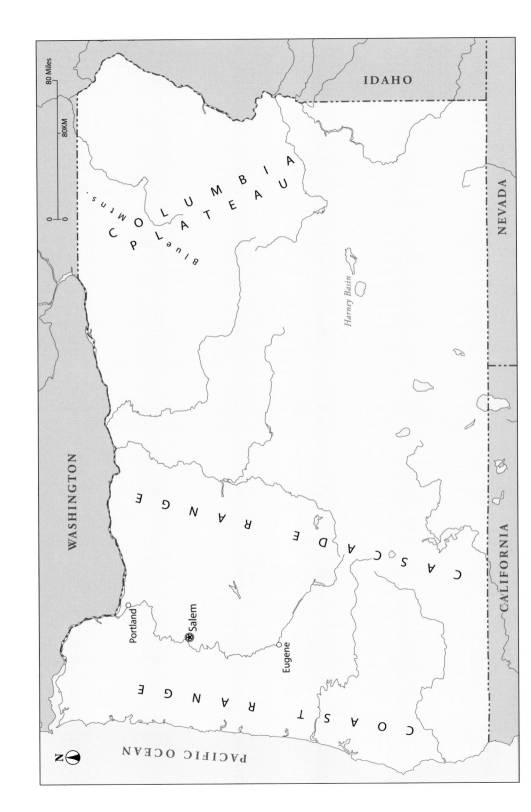

DESERT
Cacti, 99
Hedge mustard, 96
Pine, 23
Wild onions, 206

OCEAN
Fennel, 40
Glasswort, 113
Orach, 107
Rush, 209
Sea rocket, 81
Seaweeds, 14
Violet, 203

FOOTHILLS
Blackberry, 192
Blueberry, 126
Currants, 137
Dock, 172
Elderberry, 30
Fireweed, 152
Grasses, 221
Indian plum, 184
Madrone, 116
Manzanita, 120
Nettle, 199
Nightshade, 196
Oak, 130
Oregon grape, 67
Oregon myrtle, 26
Salal, 123
Serviceberry, 179
Strawberry, 181
Wild cherry, 187
Wild rose, 190

MOUNTAINS
Blueberry, 126
Bracken, 19
Camas, 217
Currants and gooseberries, 137
Hazelnut, 70
Madrone, 116
Manzanita, 120
Miner's lettuce, 149
Mint, 141
Mountain bluebells, 72
Oak, 130
Pine, 23
Salal, 123
Serviceberry, 179
Spring beauty, 147
Strawberry, 181
Violet, 203

ALPINE
American bistort, 165
Mountain bluebells, 72
Mountain sorrel, 168

RIPARIAN
Bracken, 19
Cattail, 224
Cow parsnip, 42
Mint, 141
Monkey flower, 158
Nettle, 199
Rush, 209
Veronica, 163
Watercress, 88
Wild onions, 206

URBAN AND FIELDS

Amaranth, 34
Asparagus, 213
Bittercress, 84
Blackberry, 192
Burdock, 44
Cat's ear, 54
Chicory, 51
Chickweed, 103
Dandelion, 64
Dock, 172
Elderberry, 30
Fennel, 40
Filaree, 134
Fireweed, 152
Grasses, 221
Hedge mustard, 96
Lamb's quarter, 110
Mallow, 144
Miner's lettuce, 149
Mint, 141
Mustard, 77
Nettle, 199
Nightshade, black, 196
Nipplewort, 59
Oak, 130
Pineapple weed, 49
Plantain, 160
Prickly lettuce, 56
Purslane, 176
Radish, 92
Rose, 179
Sheep sorrel, 170
Shepherd's purse, 86
Sour grass, 156
Sow thistle, 61
Thistle, 47
Violet, 203
Wild carrot, 37
Wintercress, 74

COLLECTING AND HARVESTING
WILD FOODS

Since more and more people want to learn how to "live off the land" and use wild plants for food and medicine, please practice sustainable collecting and harvesting methods.

First, always make sure it is both legal and safe for you to harvest the wild foods. Legality can usually be determined simply by asking a few questions or making a phone call. In some cases, when we're dealing with public lands, the issue of legality may be a bit more difficult to ascertain.

You also want to be safe, making sure there are not agricultural or commercial toxins near and around the plants you intend to harvest. Again, it pays in the long run to carefully observe the surroundings and to ask a few questions.

Unless it is the root that you are using for food, you should never need to uproot a plant, especially if it is only the leaves that you intend to eat. I have documented in my *Extreme Simplicity* book how I was able to extend the life of many annual weeds by carefully pinching back the leaves that I wanted to eat and then allowing the plant to grow back before picking again. Even when I believe that someone else will pull up the plant later or plow the area, I still do not uproot the plants on general principle. If I leave the plant rooted, the root system is good for the soil and the plant continues to manufacture oxygen. Various insects and birds might eat the bugs on the plant or its seeds. Let life continue.

When you are harvesting greens, snippers can be used, but usually nothing is needed but your fingernails and maybe a sharp knife. Cut what you need, don't deplete an area, and move on.

Harvesting seeds is done when the plant is at the end of its annual cycle, but there is still no reason to uproot the plant. When I harvest curly dock or lamb's quarter seed, I carefully try to get as much into my bag as possible. I know that some seed is being scattered, and that's a good thing for next season. I also know that a few seeds are still on the stalk, and that's a good thing for the birds in the area.

I nearly always harvest in an area of abundance. If there are very few specimens there, my usual course of action is to simply leave them alone.

You will note when you read this text that I advise foragers to leave the wild onions in the ground and to eat the greens. In cases of abundance, your thinning the roots will help to stimulate more growth, and that is a good thing, akin to the passive agricultural practices of the Native Americans who once exclusively lived here.

In general, foraging doesn't require many tools. You will need bags—plastic, cloth, paper—whatever is appropriate for the food item. In some cases, you harvest with buckets or tubs. Usually no other tools are needed, though I generally carry a Florian ratchet clipper for any cutting and a knife or two. I rarely need a trowel, though it comes in handy with some harvesting.

The more you forage, the more you'll realize that your best tool is your memory. You'll learn to recognize where the mushrooms grow, where the berry vines are, and the fields that will be full of chickweed next spring. And the more you know, the less you'll need to carry.

HOW MUCH WILD FOOD IS OUT THERE, ANYWAY?

Plants Everywhere, But Not All Can Be Eaten

In his book *Participating in Nature*, Thomas Elpel has created a unique chart, based on years of observation and analysis, to give a perspective on the sheer numbers of edible, medicinal, and poisonous plants. Elpel is also the author of *Botany in a Day*.

First, almost every plant with known ethnobotanical uses can be used medicinally; even some otherwise toxic plants can be used medicinally if you know the right doses and proper application. So, yes, medicine is everywhere. But nearly two-thirds of these plants are neither poisonous nor used for food for various reasons.

The extremely poisonous plants that will outright kill you are rare. And since there are so few of these deadly plants, it is not all that difficult to learn to identify them. In Oregon, for example, there is poison hemlock and death camas, which can be easily confused for something edible. Others that could cause death are various mushrooms, oleander, and tree tobacco. It is not uncommon to hear about mushroom sickness and even death.

Though there are only a few plants that are deadly poisonous, many more— perhaps five times as many plants as the very deadly ones—would make you very sick but would not normally kill you. Still, all the poisonous and toxic plants combined are just a very small percentage of all the known ethnobotanicals.

Edible plants compose maybe a quarter of the known edible, medicinal, and poisonous plants. Of the plants that we normally think of as "food plants," the overwhelming majority—maybe 70 percent or so—are primarily providing

Edible, Medicinal, and Poisonous Plants

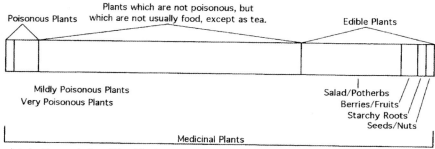

Reprinted with permission of Tom Elpel

us with greens. That is, throughout most of the year, the majority of the food that you'll obtain from the wild consists of greens: food to make salads and stir-fries and to add to soups and vegetable dishes. These are plants that by themselves will not create a filling and balanced meal, but will add vitamins and minerals to your dried beans, MREs (meals ready to eat), freeze-dried camping food, and other foods. In general, greens are not high sources of protein, fats, or carbohydrates.

Berries and fruits compose another category of wild foods. Maybe 10 to 15 percent of the wild foods you find will consist of berries or fruits, but timing is everything. Unlike greens, which you can usually find year-round, fruits and berries are typically available only seasonally, so if you want some during other times of the year, you'll need to dry them or make jams or preserves. This includes blackberries, elderberries, mulberries, and many others. They provide sugar and flavor, but like greens, you would not make a meal entirely from fruits and berries.

Then, an even smaller category of wild foods, perhaps 5 to 7 percent, consists of starchy roots, such as cattails and Jerusalem artichokes. These are great for energy, though they may not be available year-round. This is why these foods have traditionally been dried, and even powdered, and stored for use later in the year.

Another small category of wild foods consists of the seeds and nuts. This includes grass seeds, pine nuts, and acorns, among many others. It is in this small category, maybe 5 percent of wild foods, where you obtain the carbohydrates, oils, and sometimes proteins that constitute the "staff of life." Though these are not available year-round, some have a longer harvest time than others. Some may have a harvest period of as short as two weeks. Many grass seeds simply fall to the ground and are eaten by animals. Fortunately, most of these can be harvested in season and stored for later use.

ARE WILD FOODS NUTRITIOUS?

It is a common misconception that "wild foods" are neither nutritious nor tasty. Both of these points are erroneous, as anyone who has actually taken the time to identify and use wild foods can testify. I've had many new students who had been convinced about the nutritional value of wild foods but had assumed that the plants nevertheless tasted bad. Of course, a bad cook can make even the best foods unpalatable. And if you pick wild foods and don't clean them, and don't use just the tender sections, and don't prepare them properly, you'll almost certainly turn people off to wild foods.

On the other hand, my friends Pascal Baudar and Mia Wasilevich continue to use wild foods in their gourmet dishes and classes, and have proven that wild foods are not only nutritious but can be as flavorful as any foods in the finest restaurants.

For your edification, here is a chart extracted from the USDA's *Composition of Foods* to give you an idea of the nutritional content of the common wild foods.

Plant	Calories	Protein (g)	Fat (g)	Calcium (mg)	Phosphorus (mg)	Iron (mg)	Sodium (mg)	Potassium (mg)	Vitamin A (IU)	Thiamine (mg)	Riboflavin (mg)	Niacin (mg)	Vit. C (mg)	Part
Amaranth	36	3.5	0.5	267	67	3.9	—	411	6,100	0.08	0.16	1.4	80	Leaf, raw
Carob	45	4.5		352	81	2.9	35	827	14		0.4	1.89	0.2	Pods
Cattail		8%	2%											Rhizomes
Chia		20.2%		631	860	7.72	16	407	54	0.62	0.17	8.8	1.6	Seed
CHICORY TRIBE														
Chicory	20	1.8	0.3	86	40	0.9	—	420	4,000	0.06	0.1	0.5	22	Leaf, raw
Dandelion	45	2.7	0.7	187	66	3.1	76	397	14,000	0.19	0.26	—	35	Leaf, raw
Sow thistle	20	2.4	0.3	93	35	3.1	—		2,185	0.7	0.12	0.4	5	Leaf, raw
Chickweed									30 mg	0.02	1.14	0.51	375	
Dock	28	2.1	0.3	66	41	1.6	5	338	12,900	0.09	0.22	0.5	119	Leaf, raw
Fennel	28	2.8	0.4	100	51	2.7	—	397	3,500	—	—	—	31	Leaf, raw
Filaree	—	2.5	—	—	—	—	—	—	7,000	—	—	—	—	Leaf
Grass										300–500 IU	2,000 to 2,800 IU		300 to 700 mg	Leaf, raw
Jerusalem artichoke	75	2.3	0.1	14	78	3.4	—	—	20	0.2	0.06	1.3	4	Root, raw
Lamb's quarter	43	4.2	0.8	309	72	1.2	43	452	11,600	0.16	0.44	1.2	80	Leaf, raw
Mallow	37	4.4	0.6	249	69	12.7	—	—	2,190	0.13	0.2	1.0	35	Leaf
Milkweed	—	0.8	0.5	—	—	—	—	—	—	—	—	—	—	Leaf
Miner's lettuce						10% RDA			22% RDA				33% RDA	Leaf
MUSTARD FAMILY														
Mustard	31	3	0.5	183	50	3	32	377	7,000	0.12	0.22	0.8	97	Leaf
Shepherd's purse	33	4.2	0.5	208	86	4.8	—	394	1,554	0.08	0.17	0.4	36	Leaf
Watercress	19	2.2	0.3	120	60	0.2	41	330	3,191		0.12	0.2	43	Leaf
Nettle	65	5.5	0.7	481	71	1.64	4	334	2,011	—	0.16	0.38	76	Leaf

Plant	Calories	Protein (g)	Fat (g)	Calcium (mg)	Phosphorus (mg)	Iron (mg)	Sodium (mg)	Potassium (mg)	Vitamin A (IU)	Thiamine (mg)	Riboflavin (mg)	Niacin (mg)	Vit. C (mg)	Part
New Zealand spinach	19	2.2	0.3	58	46	2.6	159	795	4,300	0.04	0.17	0.6	30	Leaf, raw
Oak (acorn flour)	65% carbohydrates	6%	18%	43	103	1.21	0	712	51	0.1	0.1	2.3	0	Nut
ONION FAMILY														
Chives	28	1.8	0.3	69	44	1.7	—	250	5,800	0.08	0.13	0.5	56	Leaf, raw
Garlic	137	6.2	0.2	29	202	1.5	19	529	—	0.25	0.08	0.5	15	Clove, raw
Onion	36	1.5	0.2	51	39	1	5	231	2,000	0.05	0.05	0.4	32	Young leaf, raw
Passion fruit (per pound)				31	151	3.8	66	831	1,650				71	Fruit
Pinyon pine	635	12	60.5		604	5.2				1.28				Nut
Prickly pear	42	0.5	0.1	20	28	0.3	2	166	60	0.01	0.03	0.4	22	Fruit, raw
Purslane	21	30	1.7	0.4	103	39	3.5	—	—	2,500	0.03	0.1	0.5	Leaf & stem, raw
Rose	162	1.6		169	61	1.06	4	429	4,345		0.16	1.3	426	Fruit, raw
SEAWEED														
Dulse	—	—	3.2	296	267	—	2,085	8,060	—	—	—	—	—	Leaf
Irish moss	—	—	1.8	885	157	8.9	2,892	2,844	—	—	—	—	—	Leaf
Kelp	—	—	1.1	1,093	240	—	3,007	5,273	—	—	—	—	—	Leaf

Seaweeds

Seaweeds are, by definition, marine algae. Some are microscopic—we will address only the macroscopic seaweeds, divided into the green algae, the brown algae, and the red algae.

The author with kelp from the Pacific Ocean PHOTO BY RICK ADAMS

MARINE GREEN ALGAE

(Chlorophyta) About 5,000 species, including sea lettuce, etc. In Oregon this group is represented by sea lettuce (*Ulva lactuca*) and others.

BROWN ALGAE

(Phaeophyta) Approximately 1,000 species, including all kelps, rockweed, etc. In Oregon this group is represented by alaria (*Alaria marginata*), bull whip kelp (*Nereocystis luetkeana*), and fucus, among others.

RED ALGAE

(Rhodophyta) The most abundant seaweed in the world, with over 4,000 species, including Irish moss, dulse, laver, etc. In Oregon this group is represented by nori (*Porphyra* spp.), Turkish towel (*Chondracanthus* spp.), and others.

Use: Food (depending on species, some are eaten dried, cooked, raw, or pickled); nutrition; utility
Range: Ocean and beaches
Similarity to toxic species: None, but see Cautions
Best time: Available year-round
Status: Common
Tools needed: Bucket, gloves

PROPERTIES

Most people know seaweeds when they see them at the beach, floating in the surf or lying on the sand. They grow in a wide array of colors, sizes, and shapes. The kelps are perhaps the most conspicuous along the Oregon coast, with their long stipes and characteristic fronds. They often lie in masses on the beach.

In general, the seaweeds have leaflike fronds, stipes that resemble the stems of terrestrial plants, and holdfasts that resemble roots. Some seaweeds are very delicate, and others are very tough and almost leathery. Many have hollow sections—"floats"—which allow them to float more readily.

Others are like thin sheets of wet plastic, such as the sea lettuce. Their colors generally indicate their category of green, brown, or red marine algae.

USES

Seaweeds are not only tasty (when prepared properly), they are also very nutritious.

When I was originally researching seaweeds, I spoke with botanists, marine biologists, and even a seaweed specialist. Some believe that all seaweeds—all the thousands of varieties—are a completely nontoxic group of plants, and most agree that these are safe to consume, assuming that the water is not polluted. The more conservative viewpoint had to do with the fact that there are so many seaweeds, and not all have been studied enough to make such a blanket statement. Nevertheless, seaweeds are regarded as highly nutritious and generally edible. One hundred grams of kelp, for example, contains 1,093 mg of calcium, 240 mg of phosphorus, and 5,273 mg of potassium! And these iodine-rich foods can be used in a variety of ways.

Some—such as the sea lettuce, which actually looks like lettuce—can be washed and added raw to salads. Others are best dried and then used as a seasoning to other foods. Some seaweeds can be diced and added to soups and stews. And most can be simply dried and powdered and then used as a salt substitute or flavor enhancer.

If you live near the coast and have easy access to seaweeds, I encourage you to research the many specific seaweeds that are used for food, and—via the myriad books devoted exclusively to seaweeds—learn the various ways to prepare them. And experiment! Unless you are lost and haven't the time to experiment or research, there are many sources of information today with lots of specific recipes and methods of preparation for seaweeds.

We've made some very delicious pickles by taking the "floats" from kelp—the swollen hollow bubble at the base of each frond—and soaking them in jalapeño juice or other pickling juice. They take on the flavor of whatever they are seasoned with.

A view of the float and frond of a kelp
PHOTO BY RICK ADAMS

CAUTIONS

There are some commonsense precautions you should take if you're going to try some seaweeds: Never eat any seaweed that has been sitting on the beach rotting and attracting flies. Examine the seaweed. Never eat seaweed that has some sort of foreign growth on it. And perhaps the hardest part of all this is that you should not consume seaweed from polluted waters. This means that you have to use some common sense when collecting seaweed for food, and you should thoroughly wash any seaweed that you intend to eat.

OTHER USES OF SEAWEEDS

Seaweeds are a very diverse group that historically has been used for much more than food.

Ferns

There are 13 families of ferns. According to Dr. Leonid Enari, the young, uncurling, growing tips of ferns are edible and taste a bit nutty. These have long been steamed and served with butter or cheese, or mixed into various vegetable dishes.

Though Dr. Enari regarded the entire group of ferns as safe for food, he offered the following precautions: Cook all fiddleheads that you intend to eat, since some may be a bit toxic raw. He advised cleaning fiddleheads of hairs, if any, before cooking. Dr. Enari also advised to not eat any mature fern fronds. Though many may be safe when mature, they are not as palatable as the young fiddlehead. Thus, you need to get to know that individual fern before you would eat its mature fronds. Otherwise, eat only the fiddleheads, clean them of hairs, and cook them before eating.

There are many ferns that you will encounter in Oregon and beyond, besides what we have presented here. A few have a long history of use as food.

BRACKEN FAMILY (DENNSTAEDTIACEAE)

Among the ferns, the Bracken family contains about 11 genera and about 170 species. Its only representative in Oregon is the bracken, or brake, fern.

BRACKEN
Pteridium aquilinum

The edible fiddleheads of bracken

Use: Young uncurling shoots used for food
Range: Throughout the state, mostly in the shady areas of the mountains and canyons; not found in the deserts
Similarity to toxic species: See Cautions
Best time: Spring
Status: Somewhat common in the correct terrain
Tools needed: Clippers

PROPERTIES

Bracken can apparently be found world-wide. Ours can be found throughout the state, in pastures, hillsides, wooded areas, and even in full sun. You'll find it most commonly on the north, shady side of hillsides or shady hillsides where water seeps and where little sun gets through the canopy of whatever larger trees grow there.

The bracken leaf

The rhizomes are hairy and sprawling underground, sometimes branching. The petiole is black near the base, with dense brown hairs. The plants grow from 1 to 4 feet tall, and the overall appearance of each frond is roughly triangular; each is twice-pinnately divided.

USES

The young shoots are the edible portion and they have the appearance of the head of a fiddle, which is where the common name "fiddlehead" comes from. The young shoots will uncurl and grow into the full fern fronds. These are picked when young and could be eaten raw or cooked. I like to toss a few in salads when the fiddleheads are in season; they impart a nutty flavor.

More commonly, these are boiled or steamed and served with butter or cheese. They are easy to recognize and have gained a resurgence of popularity as more people are rediscovering wild foods. Bracken is also a good vegetable to add to soups and stews and mixed dishes.

Just carefully pinch off the tender unfolding top, and you can gently rub off the hair. Use as a nibble or cook. Do not eat the fully opened ferns.

CAUTIONS

Researchers have identified a substance called ptaquiloside in bracken fern, a known carcinogen. So is it safe to eat? It has been a food staple of Native Americans for centuries, if not millennia, and the Japanese also enjoy bracken and consider it one of the delicacies of spring. Although actual scientific data is inconclusive, there is a higher rate of intestinal cancer among Native Americans and the Japanese, and this could be linked to the use of bracken fern. Livestock have been known to be mildly poisoned by eating quantities of the raw bracken ferns. Cooking is known to remove some of the toxins, though not necessarily the ptaquiloside.

Despite this, there are many who are not so concerned about such inconclusive studies. For example, Steven Brill in his *Identifying and Harvesting Edible and Medicinal Plants* states, "I wouldn't be afraid of eating reasonable quantities of wild [bracken] fiddleheads during their short season." Another forager, Green

The mature frond of bracken

The young edible fiddlehead
PHOTO BY BARBARA KOLANDER

Deane, says, "I am willing to risk a few fiddleheads with butter once or twice a spring, which is about as often as I can collect enough in this warm place."

The final choice is up to you. For perspective, we regularly hear things far worse than the above about coffee, high-fructose corn syrup, sugar, and french fries, yet people seem to have no problem purchasing and eating these substances. That doesn't make them good for you, but eating some in moderation is not likely to be the sole cause of cancer or other illness.

LEWIS AND CLARK

Meriwether Lewis wrote about the bracken fern on January 22, 1806: "There are three species of fern in this neighbourhood the root one of which the natves [*sic*] eat; this grows very abundant in the open uplands and praries [*sic*] . . . the center of the root is divided into two equal parts by a strong flat & white ligament like a piece of thin tape—on either side of this there is a white substance which when the root is roasted in the embers is much like wheat dough and not very unlike it in flavour, though it has also a pungency which becomes more visible after you have chewed it some little time; this pungency was disagreeable to me, but the natives eat it very voraciously and I have no doubt but it is a very nutricious [*sic*] food."

OTHER FERN GROUPS

The Wood Fern family (Dryopteridaceae) consists of about 40 to 45 genera, 4 local genera, and more than 1,600 species worldwide. This family includes *Dryopteris* spp., consisting of about 100 species worldwide and commonly called Wood Fern. The family also includes *Polystichum* spp., with about 175 species worldwide and commonly referred to as Sword Fern.

The Cliff Fern family (*Woodsiaceae*) consists of 15 genera and about 700 species worldwide. One species sometimes eaten is lady fern (*Athyrium filix-femina*) and 2 varieties.

The Deer Fern family (*Blechnaceae*) consists of 9 genera and about 250 species worldwide. Common locally, and sometimes eaten, is deer fern (*Blechnum spicant*).

Gymnosperms

This is a class of plants whose naked seeds are formed in cones, as with a pine cone, or on stalks, as with Ephedra. The members of this group include the cycadophytes, conifers, ginkgo, and ephedras.

PINE FAMILY (PINACEAE)

The Pine family is said to supply about half the world's lumber needs. The family consists of 10 genera and 193 species. There are 94 species of *Pinus* in the Northern Hemisphere, and at least 15 are known to grow in the wild in Oregon.

PINE
Pinus spp.

A view of pine needles and cones PHOTO BY RICK ADAMS

Use: Needles for tea and spice; nuts for food
Range: Various species are found in the mountains and throughout the state. Often planted in urban areas.
Similarity to toxic species: None
Best time: Nuts in the fall; needles can be collected anytime.
Status: Common in certain localities
Tools needed: Clippers for needles

The unshelled pine nuts, left, and shelled pine nuts, right

PROPERTIES

Pines are fairly widespread trees, with species growing along the coast, in the Cascades, on the eastern slopes, and in bogs, with some preferring burned-over areas. There are 94 species in the Northern Hemisphere. In Oregon we find coast pine (*Pinus contorta*) with needles mostly in 2s; western yellow pine (*P. ponderosa*) with needles mostly in 3s and found mostly in eastern Cascades; *P. flexis* (needles in 5s, mostly eastern Oregon); *P. albicaulis* (needles in 5s, through the Cascades); limber pine (*P. lambertiana*) with needles in 5s and found mostly in southwest Oregon; and western white pine (*P. monticola*) with needles in 5s and found in the Olympic Mountains and the Cascades.

Pines are one of the easier conifers to identify: All the needles are "bundled" at their base into groups of 1 to 5 with papery sheaths; each such cluster is called a fascicle.

The pines in Oregon can range from about 30 feet tall (the coast pine) up to about 200 feet tall (the western yellow pine). You look for the bundled needles and you look for the cones. The cones are often tightly spiraled with a variety of scale types. As the cones mature, they open up to reveal a pine nut under each scale. Each pine nut has a thin black shell and an oily white inside.

USES

Though there are a few potential foods with the pines, it is mostly the seeds that will provide you with food that is both substantial and palatable.

The cones mature and open in the fall. As the scales open sufficiently, the seeds drop to the ground, where they can be collected if you're there at the right time and beat the animals to them. The seeds may drop over a period of 2 weeks to a month. One of the best methods to harvest is to lay sheets under the trees to catch the seeds so they're not lost in the grass. The seeds are then shelled and eaten as a snack, added to soups, or mashed and added to biscuits or pancakes.

I have taken the not-fully-mature cones and put them into the fire, carefully watching them so they don't burn. The idea is to open the scales and then get the seeds. However, I do not recommend this method.

The tender needles can also be collected and brewed into a tea. Put the needles in a covered container, and boil at a low temperature for a few minutes. Your tea is vitamin C rich and very aromatic and tasty—that is, if you enjoy the flavor of a Christmas tree, which is what you'll smell like after drinking it. It's very good.

Yes, we have all heard of eating the cambium layer of pine trees. I once read an article titled "Spaghetti That Grows on Trees," and it showed a woman who had peeled off the cambium layer of the bark (the inner layer)

Forager note: Some of the very long needles of certain pines are excellent for coiled baskets.

and had supposedly cooked strips of it to make a wild spaghetti. She was actually smiling in the picture, which was my clue that she hadn't actually eaten any of this "spaghetti." I regard this as a "survival food," meaning it could be worth all the work involved if you're actually near-starving. You most likely would not break into a smile if you were eating such a fibrous and resinous food.

Magnoliids

Formerly, this was considered a part of the category of dicots (now called eudicots). The floral parts of the magnoliids are generally spirally arranged or in 3s.

LAUREL FAMILY (LAURACEAE)

The Laurel family has 54 genera and 3,500 species worldwide. In Oregon this family is only represented by the Oregon myrtle.

OREGON MYRTLE (a.k.a. CALIFORNIA BAY)
Umbellularia californica

The linear leaves of the Oregon myrtle and an unripe fruit

Use: Leaves for tea and spice; nuts for food

Range: Almost exclusively along streams; sometimes planted in urban areas. Though far more common in California, it does grow in western Oregon along the coast.

Similarity to toxic species: The leaves resemble oleander; however, oleander lacks the strong fragrance of the bay leaf.

Best time: Leaves can be collected anytime; nuts mature in October and November.

Status: Generally restricted to riparian areas

Tools needed: None

PROPERTIES

Oregon myrtle is primarily a riparian tree, though it can be found as a shrub in the chaparral and occasionally planted in urban areas as a landscaping tree.

The leaves are very reminiscent of a lanceolate eucalyptus leaf, except these leaves are darker, and their aroma (especially when crushed) is quite distinctive. The young wood has a darker hue, and the bark becomes smoother and lighter as the plant matures.

The nuts are first green, and then darken before they fall to the ground, somewhat resembling an olive. Once the mushy flesh is removed, there is a thin shell and then the meat inside.

The leaf and fruit of the Oregon myrtle

A bowl of the harvested bay nuts, the nuts of the Oregon myrtle

USES

Collect the nuts from the ground in autumn. Remove the flesh and thin shells and then, to make more palatable, dry or roast. You could also try boiling the shelled nuts. The nuts could also be dried and ground into a flour and used in various pastry products.

The leaves can be used fresh or dried to make a pleasant drink. Add a leaf to your canteen of water, shake the canteen, and enjoy. Or add a leaf to your cup, add hot water, and then drink when it's cool enough. It's a delicious tea. The tea is sometimes drunk to relieve stomach pains from overeating or indigestion.

The leaves of this plant have also long been used to repel bugs from bags of rice or beans. This is a good practice at home and when traveling. Simply add a few dried leaves to a container of rice or other grain. The strong aroma tends to deter bugs.

Though not a direct food source, archery is one of the ways that indigenous peoples hunted for meat. The bay tree's wood is a top-quality wood for making bows.

CAUTIONS

This is not the same leaf as the European bay more typically sold in the spice sections of stores. Oregon myrtle is much stronger, and some people have a negative reaction to using the leaves for tea, such as headaches. Try just a little at first to make sure you have no reactions. In fact, when you crush and smell a fresh leaf, the aroma is so pungent that it can cause some people to have headaches.

Forager note: Though some people have said that their headache was cured by inhaling the fumes from a freshly crushed bay leaf, as many others have said that inhaling the strong fragrance causes a headache.

Eudicots

This category was formerly referred to as dicots. The sprouts begin with 2 cotyledons, and the flower parts generally occur in 4s or 5s. All families in this category are arranged alphabetically by their Latin name.

MUSKROOT FAMILY (ADOXACEAE)

This family has 5 genera and about 200 species worldwide. Only 2 of the genera are represented in Oregon.

ELDERBERRY
Sambucus spp.

Elder flower and fruit PHOTO BY HELEN NYERGES

There are 2 common species of *Sambucus* in Oregon and a few varieties and sub-varieties: blue elderberry, *S. caerulea*, formerly *S. glauca* and sometimes *S. nigra* subsp. *caerulea*; *S. nigra* with black fruit, sometime described as *S. racemosa*; and red elderberry, *S. racemosa*, formerly *S. callicarpa*. As botanists continue to redefine each of these elderberries, it's likely that a few new varieties or subvarieties will be defined in the next few years, and everything here in Latin will be wrong or obsolete.

Use: Flowers for tea and food; berries for "raisins," jam, jelly, juice
Range: Throughout the state in the mountains, urban fringe, and generally most environments
Similarity to toxic species: See Cautions
Best time: Early spring for flowers; early summer for fruit
Status: Common
Tools needed: Clippers for flowers; clippers and good, sturdy bucket for berries

A view of the elder flower

PROPERTIES

There are 20 species of *Sambucus* worldwide. Elder can be found throughout the state, in the drier regions, along streams, and in the higher mountain regions. They are generally small trees, with oppositely arranged, pinnately divided leaves with a terminal leaflet. Each leaflet has a fine serration along its edge.

The plant is often inconspicuous but is very obvious when it blossoms in its many yellowish-white flower clusters in the spring. By early summer the fruits develop in clusters, which are often drooping from the weight.

USES

Remember the Boy Scout saying: Black and blue is good for you, red as a brick will get you sick!

EDIBILITY

The blue berries, rich in vitamin A and with fair amounts of potassium and calcium, can be eaten raw or can be mashed and blended with applesauce for a unique dessert, especially if you are using wild apples. The berries can also be used for making wines, jellies, jams, and pies.

Though some of the Indian tribes of Oregon ate the red berries when cooked, there are people today who get sick from the red ones. I do not advise that you eat red elderberries at all; however, if you decide to try them, cook them well and sample only a little bit at first to see how your body reacts.

A bowl of the collected mature fruit of the elder is ready to be processed into juice.

Nyerges with a bundle of the long pieces of elder bark. They are useful for weaving mats or used for tinder in fire-starting. PHOTO BY ALAN HALCON

Wild-food researcher Pascal Baudar likes to dry and powder the blue fruit and sprinkle it over ice cream. The whole flower cluster can be gathered, dipped in batter, and fried, producing a wholesome pancake. Try dipping the flower clusters in a batter of the sweet yellow cattail pollen (see Cattail) and frying it like pancakes. It's delicious!

Another method to use the flowers is to remove them from the clusters and the little stems, and then mix with flour in a proportion of 50-50 for baking pastries, breads, biscuits, and more.

MEDICINE

The flowers also make a traditional Appalachian tea that was said to be useful for colds, fevers, and headaches. According to Dr. James Adams, author of *Healing with Medicinal Plants of the West*, a tea made from elderberry flowers was used by indigenous peoples to cure colds, flus, and fevers.

The long, straight stems of elder have a soft pith and have historically been hollowed out and used for such things as pipe stems, blowguns, flutes, and straws for stoking a fire.

Forager note: If you don't want your fruit to get all smashed and crushed, don't collect in a bag. Collect in a basket or bucket, and don't pack too many into the bucket.

The bark of the older stalks was removed by indigenous peoples and woven into mats and even clothing. Because it is soft and fibrous, this old shredded bark is also an excellent fire tinder.

CAUTIONS

Be sure to cook the fruit before eating it, and avoid the red berries entirely. While not everyone will get sick from eating the dark purple or black berries raw, they can cause severe nausea in some people. Therefore, cook all fruit before using for drinks or other dishes.

Do not consume the leaves, as this will result in sickness.

RECIPE

Elderberry Sauce

This simple sauce goes well with any game (such as duck), but feel free to try it with chicken too!

1 pound elderberries (freeze the clusters first, crush them lightly with your hands, and the berries will fall easily)

1 large sweet onion or 7–8 scallions

⅔ cup red wine vinegar

¾ cup sugar or honey

1 teaspoon grated ginger

A couple of cloves

½ teaspoon of salt, or to taste

Place the berries in a pot and squeeze them with your hand first to release the juice. Add the remaining ingredients and bring to a boil for 10 minutes. Strain the liquid through a sieve.
Return the liquid to the pot, bring to a simmer, and reduce until you have achieved the right consistency (like a commercial steak sauce). You can prepare it in advance and keep it in the fridge for many days.

—RECIPE FROM PASCAL BAUDAR

AMARANTH FAMILY (AMARANTHACEAE)

The Amaranth family has 75 genera and 900 species worldwide. There are about 20 genera of this family in Oregon. Of the members of the *Amaranthus* genus in Oregon, *A. retroflexus* seems to be the most common of about 9 species.

AMARANTH
Amaranthus spp.

Oscar Duardo shows the amaranths he grows in his community garden for seed and leaf.

Rick Adams inspects the large leaves of one of the erect cultivated amaranths.

Use: Seeds for soup or pastries and bread products; leaves can be eaten raw or cooked.

Range: Amaranth is widespread. Though it is most common in the disturbed soils of farms, gardens, fields, and urban lots, you can usually find some amaranth in open areas where there is some moisture, even seasonally.

Similarity to toxic species: Some ornamentals resemble amaranth. Some toxic plants superficially resemble amaranth, such as the nightshades (e.g., *Solanum nigrum*). Individual jimsonweed leaves (*Datura* spp.) have been confused for amaranth leaves. Generally, once the amaranth begins to flower and go to seed, this confusion is diminished.

Best time: Spring for the leaves; late fall for the seeds

Status: Common

Tools needed: Tight-weave bag for collecting the seeds

PROPERTIES

Though there are many species of *Amaranthus*, *A. retroflexus* is most common in Oregon.

Amaranth is an annual. The ones with erect stalks can grow up to 3 feet and taller, depending on the species. Some are more branched and are lower to the ground. When young, the root of one of the common varieties, *A. retroflexus*, is red, and the bottoms of the young leaves are purple. The leaves of *A. retroflexus* are oval shaped, alternate, and glossy. Other *Amaranthus* leaves can be ovate to linear.

The plant produces flowers, but they are not conspicuous. They are formed in spikelike clusters, and numerous shiny black seeds develop when the plant matures in late summer. The plant is common and widespread in urban areas, fields, farms, backyards, and roadsides.

USES

Amaranth is a versatile plant with edible parts available throughout its growing season.

The young leaves and tender stems of late winter and spring can

The red root of the *Amaranthus retroflexus*

The erect *Amaranth hybridus* is often grown in gardens.

be eaten raw in salads, but because there is often a hint of bitterness, they are best mixed with other greens. Young and tender stems are boiled in many parts of the world and served with butter or cheese as a simple vegetable. Older leaves get bitter and should be boiled into a spinach-like dish, or added to soups, stews, stir-fries, etc. In Mexico leaves are sometimes dried and made into a flour, which is added to tamales and other dishes.

Forager note: Amaranths are a diverse group. Some have an erect stalk, some are highly branched, and some are prostrate.

Amaranthus retroflexus, showing the red root

The mature seed of wild amaranth is black, tiny, and shiny.

Amaranth begins to produce seeds in late summer, and once the seeds are black, they can be harvested. The entire plant is generally already very withered and dried up by the time you're harvesting. The seeds are added to soups, bread batter, and pastry products.

The seeds and leaves are very nutritious, no doubt part of the reason this plant was so revered in the old days. One hundred grams of the seed contain about 358 calories, 247 mg of calcium, 500 mg of phosphorus, and 52.5 mg of potassium. The seed offers a nearly complete balance of essential amino acids, including lysine and methionine.

The leaf is also very nutritious, being high in calcium and potassium. One hundred grams, about ½ cup, of amaranth leaf has 267 to 448 mg of calcium, 411 to 617 mg of potassium, 53 to 80 mg of vitamin C, 4,300 mcg (micrograms) of beta carotene, and 1,300 mcg of niacin. This volume of leaf contains about 35 calories.

Historical note: The seed and leaf of this plant played a key part in the diet of precolonial Mexicans. The seeds would be mixed with honey or blood and shaped into images of their gods, and these images were then eaten as a "communion." Sound familiar? After the Spanish invaded Mexico, they made it illegal to grow the amaranth plant, with the justification that it was a part of "pagan rituals."

CARROT (OR PARSLEY) FAMILY (APIACEAE)

The Carrot family has about 300 genera worldwide, with about 3,000 species. In Oregon there are over 30 genera of this family. Many are cultivated for food, spice, and medicine, but some are highly toxic. Never eat anything that looks carrot- or parsley-like if you haven't positively identified it.

WILD CARROT
Daucus carota

A patch of wild carrots

The mature wild carrot flower umbel often folds in like this, giving the appearance of a bird's nest.

On each flower cluster of wild carrots, you will find one purple flower in the middle. PHOTO BY ALGIE AU

There are about 20 species of *Daucus* worldwide, and 2 are found in Oregon.

Use: The root can be dug and used like farm-grown carrots, but they are tougher. Seeds are sometimes used as a spice.

Range: Not a native, but can be found throughout much of Oregon, often in disturbed or poor soils and along roadsides

Similarity to toxic species: See Cautions

Best time: For a more-tender root, dig before the plant flowers.

Status: Found sporadically throughout Oregon

Tools needed: Shovel

PROPERTIES

If you've ever grown carrots in your garden, you will recognize the wild carrot in the wild, except it will typically be smaller. Smell the crushed leaf, and scrape a bit of the root and smell it. Does it smell like carrot? The root of the wild carrot is white, not orange, and if you scratch it, you'll get that very characteristic carrot aroma.

The leaves are pinnately dissected, with the leaflet segments linear to lanceolate—just like the leaves of a garden

The wild carrot root is white, not orange. When you scratch it, it gives off the obvious carrot aroma.

carrot. The flowers are formed in umbels of white flowers, with a tiny central flower that is purple. As the umbel matures, it closes up and has the appearance of a bird's nest.

USES

The roots can be dug, washed, and eaten like garden carrots, though they are usually tough. This was one of the first wild foods that I learned to use. It was always a feeling of great mystery and pleasure to dig into a wild field and pull up one of these white roots. Was it a farm carrot gone feral? Probably. It still woke up some inner distant memory of "hunter-gatherer."

Sometimes I simply peel the outer part of the taproot and discard the very tough inner core. The roots—if tender enough—can be sliced thin and added to salads. They're probably best added to soups, stews, and various cooked dishes. Generally when I have found these, even the outer layer of the root is a bit tough, so I slice it thin and cook it. It adds a good flavor to soups, though it lacks the carotene of commercial carrots.

The seeds of the mature plant can be collected and used as a seasoning, to taste.

CAUTIONS

The Carrot family contains some very good food and spices; however, make absolutely certain that you have a carrot and not poison hemlock, which are both members of this family. The wild carrot plant has that very distinctive carrot aroma and has fine hairs on the stalk. Poison hemlock lacks the hairs, and usually you will see mottled purple markings on the stem.

Gary Gonzales holds a leaf of the wild hemlock plant, which has a similar configuration to wild carrot.

Poison hemlock has purple blotches on the lower stalk, and it lacks the obvious carrot aroma.

FENNEL
Foeniculum vulgare

Nathaniel Schleimer examines a fennel plant.

Keith Farrar inspects a mature fennel stalk with last season's dry stalks still present.

Fennel is the only species of the *Foeniculum* genus.

Use: Leaf and stalk eaten raw or cooked; seed for tea or seasoning

Range: Widespread as an "invasive species" along the coast; common locally in urban lots and fields. Well established west of the Cascades.

Similarity to toxic species: Fennel has needlelike leaves and smells like licorice, so you really shouldn't confuse it with anything toxic. However, this family contains some poisonous and toxic members, so be certain you're picking fennel before eating it.

Best time: Spring for the young shoots; summer or fall for the seeds

Status: Widespread and common in certain localities

Tools needed: None

PROPERTIES

Fennel is a perennial from Europe that is very common along the Pacific coast and in wet areas. It is abundant in certain areas and generally considered invasive.

The plant begins to produce its ferny leaves in the spring. The finely dissected leaves—all composed of needlelike segments—give the plant a ferny appearance. The base of each leaf clasps the stalk with a flared base, similar to the base of a celery stalk. The unmistakable characteristic is the strong licorice aroma of the crushed leaf. A blind person should be able to identify this plant by the strong aroma.

The plants begin to appear in winter and early spring. They first establish a ferny, bushy, 2- to 3-foot broad base. By spring and early summer, the flower stalks rise to a height of 6 feet (higher in ideal conditions). The entire plant has a slightly bluish-green cast, due to a thin, waxy coating on the stalks and leaves. The yellow flowers form in large distinctive umbels.

USES

Young fennel leaves and peeled stalks are great to eat as a trail snack when you're thirsty and hungry. When the plant first sprouts up in the spring, you can eat the entire tender and succulent base, somewhat like you'd eat celery. As it sends up its stalk, but before the plant has flowered, the stalk is still tender and can be easily cut into segments. These tender segments are hollow and round in the cross section and can be used like celery for dipping, or cooked like asparagus and served with cheese and butter.

Later, as the plant grows taller, you can eat the tender leaves and stems, chopped up in salads or added to soups and stews. It gets

A view of the fennel plant with the seed stalks

The umbel of dried fennel seeds

a bit fibrous as it matures but can be diced up and added to many dishes. The older lower leaves can also be dried, and the crumbled herb can then be added to soups and other dishes. It adds a sweet spiciness to the dishes in which it is used. If you don't care for licorice, you probably won't care for fennel.

When the seeds mature, they can be made into a licorice-flavored tea. Just put 5 or 6 seeds into a cup and add hot water. The seeds alone can be chewed as a breath freshener or used to season other dishes.

Fennel is widely considered a pest in Oregon (and beyond) because it grows so thick in some areas that it chokes out the native vegetation. This is one of those ideal plants to grow in the lazy man's garden, but don't plant it unless you really like it! It seems to take care of itself, does well in sun or shade, and continues to arise year after year from its roots, providing seed and leaf for your meals, and perhaps habitat for a few local birds.

COW PARSNIP
Heracleum maximum, formerly *H. lanatum*

The cow parsnip plant in flower PHOTO BY BARRY BRECKLING

There are about 80 species of *Heracleum* worldwide; 2 species are found in Oregon.

Use: The tender parts of the stalk are edible.
Range: Prefers lowlands, stream banks, and wetlands
Similarity to toxic species: See Cautions
Best time: Spring
Status: Somewhat widespread, especially in the western part of the state
Tools needed: Knife

PROPERTIES

This is a robust plant, an obvious member of the Carrot or Parsley family because of the white flowers that are clustered in umbels. The flowers are composed of 5 sepals, 5 petals, 5 stamens, and 1 pistil.

The plant can grow up to 10 feet tall, though 4 to 6 feet seems to be the norm. It produces leaves with 3 large coarsely toothed lobes, very much palmate, almost like maple leaves. The plant has a stout hollow stalk. There is also a carrot-like taproot.

The plant is most commonly found in mountain meadows and moist areas. It's a typically conspicuous plant, which you cannot help but notice.

A view of the cow parsnip in flower and the leaf PHOTO BY SIVINSKI

USES

The root is sometimes cooked and eaten, with a flavor that has been compared to rutabaga. Eating the root is said to be good for the digestive system.

The tender stalk can be peeled and eaten raw, though it is really better when you cook it. The young stalks are best, and the flavor is usually compared to celery.

The dried and powdered leaves have been used as a seasoning for other foods, generally as

Note the texture of the cow parsnip stem. PHOTO BY ZOYA AKULOVA

you'd use salt. You can experiment and see if this appeals to you. The leaves have also been dried and burned and the ash used as a seasoning.

Native Americans of the area had many uses for the cow parsnip plant, besides eating the young peeled stems. They would make the plant into a poultice to treat sores and bruises. The hollow stems were also used as drinking straws as well as flutes.

CAUTIONS

Although this is one of the easiest members of the Carrot family to identify, the family does contain some deadly members, so do not eat any part of this plant until you've made positive identification.

Also, the young stalk with its fine hairs is typically peeled before eating because the surface of the stalk causes a dermatitis reaction in some people.

SUNFLOWER FAMILY (ASTERACEAE)

Worldwide, the Sunflower family has about 1,500 genera and about 23,000 species! This is the largest family in Oregon.

The Jepson Manual divides this very large family into 14 groups. Most of the plants addressed here are in Group 7, described as having ligulate heads, 5-lobed ligules (5 teeth per petal), and generally containing milky sap when broken. When I was studying botany in the 1970s, my teachers described this group as "the Chicory Tribe," a much more descriptive title than the unimaginative "Group 7." According to Dr. Leonid Enari, the Chicory Tribe contains no poisonous members and is a worthy group for further edibility research. I have eaten many of the other members of this group not listed here, though generally they require extensive boiling and water changing to render edible and palatable.

GROUP 4

BURDOCK
Arctium minus and *A. lappa*

A view of the burdock leaf, first year PHOTO BY LOUIS-M. LANDRY

There are 10 species of *Arctium* throughout Europe, and 3 are found in Oregon.

Use: The root, stems, and leaves can be eaten.

Range: Not a native, but can be found throughout the state, especially in the Great Basin area. Prefers old orchards, waste areas, and fields.

Similarity to toxic species: Resembles a rhubarb leaf

Best time: The best time to dig the root is in the first year's growth.

Status: Relatively common

Tools needed: Shovel

The typical configuration of the burdock leaves

PROPERTIES

The first time I saw wild burdock on my grandfather's farm, I thought I was looking at a rhubarb plant, though the stalk was not red and celery-like, as with rhubarb.

The first-year plant produces a rosette of rhubarb-type leaves; in ideal soil, the second-year plant produces a stalk 6 to 9 feet tall. Both of these species are similar, with *A. lappa* growing a bit taller.

The spiny-hooked burs of the burdock contain the seeds. PHOTO BY JEAN PAWEK

The leaves are heart shaped (cordate) or broadly ovate. The leaves are conspicuously veined. The first-year leaves are large and up to 2 feet in length. In the second season, the plant sends up a flower stalk with similar, but smaller, leaves. The purple to white flowers, compressed in bur-like heads, bloom in July and August. The seed containers are spiny-hooked burs that stick to socks and pants like Velcro.

Burdock's root looks like an elongated carrot, except that it is white inside with a brownish-gray skin that is peeled away before eating. You sometimes find this root in the markets sold as "gobo."

USES

The first-year roots can be dug, washed, and eaten once peeled. They are usually simmered in water until tender and cooked with other vegetables. In Russia the roots have been used as potato substitutes when potatoes aren't available. Roots can be peeled and sliced into thin pieces and sautéed or cooked with vegetables. I also eat young tender roots diced into salad, and I find them very tasty.

The root, peeled and sliced, is ready to be cooked in soup.

Leaves can be eaten once boiled; in some cases, two boilings are necessary, depending on your taste. Try to get them very young. Peeled leaf stems can be eaten raw or cooked. The erect flower stalks, collected before the flowers open, can be peeled of their bitter green skin and then dried or cooked, though these tend to be much more fibrous than the leaf stems. Still, most people prefer to eat only the root of burdock.

An analysis of the root (100 grams, or ½ cup) shows 50 mg of calcium, 58 mg of phosphorus, and 180 mg of potassium. Tea of the roots is said to be useful in treating rheumatism.

Herbalists all over the world use burdock: The roots and seeds are a soothing demulcent, tonic, and alterative (restorative to normal health). According to Linda Sheer, who grew up in rural Kentucky, burdock leaf was the best herbal treatment that her people used for rattlesnake bites. Two leaves are simmered in milk and given to the victim to drink. The burdock helps to counteract the effects of the venom. The body experiences both shock and calcium loss as a result of a rattlesnake bite. The lactose in the milk offsets the calcium loss and prevents or reduces shock.

You can also take the large burdock leaves and wrap fish and game in them before roasting in the coals of a fire pit. Foods cooked this way are mildly seasoned by the leaves.

THISTLE
Cirsium spp.

The young rosette of the thistle plant

Worldwide, there are about 200 species of the *Cirsium* genus. At least 18 are found in Oregon.

Use: Edible stems
Range: Found throughout the state in most areas
Similarity to toxic species: None
Best time: Spring
Status: Widespread
Tools needed: Knife, clippers, bag

PROPERTIES

There are many species of thistle, all with very similar appearances. Thistle normally reaches 4 to 5 feet at maturity. They can be either perennial or biennial herbs.

Thistle leaves are alternate leaves, prickly or spiny, and generally toothed. They're about 8 inches long at maturity. Thistle flowers are clustered in bristly heads. They are crimson, purple, pink, and occasionally white. The lower half of

The flowering thistle shows its relationship to artichoke.

the flower heads are covered with spiny bracts, resembling its cultivated relative the artichoke.

USES

When the plant is young and no flower stalk has emerged, the root can be dug, cooked, and eaten. These are starchy roots, mild-flavored, and as the plant flowers, the root becomes tough and fibrous. If you want to try eating the roots, you want to search in the spring in rich soil. If the soil and the timing are not right, the root is too tough to eat.

My favorite part of the thistle is the stalk, cut before the flowers develop while the stalk is still tender. The stalk is very tasty raw—somewhat sweet and reminiscent of celery.

To harvest, I typically take my knife and carefully cut off the prickly leaves, and then I am able to cut the stalk. These tender stalks can be added to salads, baked, boiled, sautéed, or added to other foods.

In general, before you eat the stalk, you should scrape off its outer fibrous layer.

Another possible food source with the thistle are the very young sprouts, and timing is the key. If there have been rains and the seeds are sprouting under the previous season's plants, you should be able to collect many of these. I like them raw, but they are good in cooked dishes too. The best are those that are the very youngest, with just the first two cotyledons, and the youngest pair of leaves that have not yet grown prickly.

GROUP 5

PINEAPPLE WEED
Matricaria discoidea, formerly *M. matricarioides*

A view of the low-growing pineapple weed plant

There are 7 species of *Matricaria* worldwide, with 4 found in Oregon.

Use: The entire plant can be used for a pleasant tea.
Range: Widespread, preferring hard soils
Similarity to toxic species: Superficially resembles very young poison hemlock
Best time: Spring, when the flowers are present
Status: Prefers hard-packed soils
Tools needed: Sharp knife or scissors, bag

PROPERTIES
This is a relative of the chamomile plant, so if you've ever grown chamomile, you have a good idea of the general appearance of pineapple weed. You most commonly find the plant growing in rock-hard soil, maybe where cars have driven, the type of soil where you cannot easily stick a shovel.

This is an annual herb that can arise as much as 8 inches but is usually less than that—typically 3 or 4 inches tall. The leaves are finely divided into short, narrow linear segments, which are alternately arranged and glabrous (not hairy). The flower heads are formed at the ends or tips of the branches and are cone shaped and small, about ½ inch in length. There are no ray flowers on the pineapple weed, meaning no petals.

When you crush the leaves and particularly the greenish flower head, you get a distinctive aroma of pineapple, hence the name. Some will find the aroma suggestive of common chamomile.

A view of the pineapple weed plant with hikers in background for size comparison

USES

I have had the young heads served as a garnish in salads and even tossed into soups. But most of the time, the plant is used to make a pleasant beverage. Pineapple weed is closely related to chamomile, and, according to Dr. Enari, its active chemistry is a bit weaker than chamomile. Nevertheless, it is used medicinally in all the ways you'd use chamomile, such as for its calming effect. Additionally, many people commonly use it as a beverage simply because they enjoy its flavor.

The whole aboveground herb can be cut and infused to make a pleasant tea. Or you can snip off just the flowers to make an even more flavorful beverage. Some people will find the flavor of the entire herb a bit bitter, and so we can say this is an acquired taste. If you want to take the time, you can just pick the flowers and brew them, and this doesn't have the bitterness that you'll find with the leaf.

You can dry this herb for later out-of-season use, or you can use it fresh when it's in season. Drink plain or sweetened, as you wish.

CAUTIONS

Since these low-growing plants are so close to the ground, be sure to wash them well before using.

GROUP 7 (or 8, depending on which botanist you follow)

CHICORY
Cichorium intybus

The flowering chicory plant PHOTO BY RICK ADAMS

There are about 6 species of *Cichorium* worldwide; only this one is found in Oregon. You can occasionally find the related endive, which is not common, near gardens or farms where it went feral.

Use: Root for beverage and food; greens raw or cooked
Range: Widespread; found especially in the disturbed soils of farms, fields, and gardens
Similarity to toxic species: None
Best time: Spring
Status: Common locally
Tools needed: Digging tool for digging roots

PROPERTIES
The chicory plant grows upright, typically 3 to 5 feet tall, with prominent sky-blue flowers. Look carefully at the flower—each petal is divided into 5 teeth, typical of the Chicory Tribe of the Sunflower family. Each leaf will produce a bit

A view of the chicory leaf, showing the leaf attachment PHOTO BY RICK ADAMS

The beautiful sky-blue chicory flower. Note the 5 teeth on each petal. PHOTO BY RICK ADAMS

of milky sap when cut. The older upper leaves on the stalk very characteristically clasp the stem at the base.

This is a perennial from Europe that is now widespread in parts of Oregon, mostly in fields, gardens, disturbed soils, and along roadsides.

USES

This is another of those incredibly nutritious plants with multiple uses. The leaves can be added to salads, preferably the very young leaves. If you don't mind a bit of bitterness, the older leaves can be added to salads too. The leaves can be cooked like spinach and added to a variety of dishes, such as soups, stews, and egg dishes.

Some chicory roots

Gary Gonzales shows a can of coffee blended with chicory root.

Chicory roots are also either boiled and buttered or sliced and added to stews and soups. Roots in rich soil tend to be less woody and fibrous.

Chicory roots have long been used as a substitute for coffee or as a coffee extender. Dig and wash the roots, and then dry them, grind them, and roast them until they are brown. Use as you would regular coffee grounds, alone or as a coffee extender. Incidentally, you can make this same coffee substitute/extender with the roots of dandelion and sow thistle.

Note: The entire Chicory Tribe of the Sunflower family contains no poisonous members, though many are bitter. Some are very bitter! These are generally tender-leafed plants with milky sap and "dandelion-like" flowers, each petal of which usually has 5 teeth at the tip.

CAT'S EAR
Hypochaeris radicata

The cat's ear plant in flower

A view of the entire cat's ear plant

There are about 60 species of *Hypochaeris* worldwide, with just 2 found in Oregon: this one, also known as "rough cat's ear," and *H. glabra*, also known as "smooth cat's ear."

Use: Leaves and shoots eaten
Range: This plant likes lawns and fields and is found in the same environments where dandelion grows.
Similarity to toxic species: Though this can be easily confused with other species when not in flower, none are toxic.
Best time: Spring
Status: Widespread throughout the state; most common west of the Cascades
Tools needed: Collecting bag

PROPERTIES
When seen for the first time, most folks think they are looking at a dandelion, though it's not quite a dandelion. Yes, cat's ear is found in pretty much the same environments as dandelion: lawns, fields, along trails, and in disturbed soils. I've seen whole lawns covered in just this plant.

The plant will grow into a rosette of the dandelion-like leaves. In some cases, the leaves more closely resemble prickly lettuce. However, the lobes of the cat's ear leaves are not sharply defined as with dandelion; rather, they are somewhat rounded, as you can see in the photo. The leaves of cat's ear are also a bit tougher than dandelion, almost leathery in some cases.

The flower stalk arises very much dandelion-style, with a similar composite flower. Because this plant is a member of the Chicory Tribe of the Sunflower family, you will see slight milkiness when you break the stem, in addition to the 5 tiny teeth at the tip of each yellow flower petal.

The rosette of the cat's ear plant

USES

The young leaves can be added to various raw or cooked dishes. Only the very youngest leaves should be used for salads, as the leaves develop a toughness as they mature. The raw leaves are bitter, but not terribly so, and they are best mixed with other greens.

Many of the leaves can be collected, then washed and used as a spinach dish. They are OK cooked alone, but much better when mixed with other greens and vegetables.

A closer look at the leaves of cat's ear

John Kallas, author of *Edible Wild Plants*, describes collecting the young, tender shoots, about 3 to 4 inches. He steams these and serves them like asparagus, though they are not as tender. In fact, a plate of cat's ear shoots looks very much like a plate of asparagus. You can then serve this with your favorite sauce, or try topping them with butter or cheese.

PRICKLY LETTUCE
Lactuca serriola, et al.

The rosette of young prickly lettuce leaves

There are about 100 species of *Lactuca* worldwide, with at least 5 found in Oregon. *Lactuca serriola*, a European native, is probably the most abundant and widespread.

Use: Young leaves, raw or cooked
Range: Most commonly found in gardens, disturbed soils, along trails, and on edges of farms
Similarity to toxic species: None
Best time: Early spring
Status: Widespread

Forager note: One of the common names for this plant is "compass plant." When the plant is mature, the edges of the leaves tend to point to the sun as the sun moves across the sky. This is probably a mechanism to stop water loss. While this is by no means as accurate as using a compass, it could help you determine directions with a bit of figuring.

PROPERTIES

Prickly lettuce is a very common annual plant that you can find just about anywhere, hidden in plain view. Yes, you've seen it, but it likely blended into the landscape. It's mostly an "urban weed," though occasionally you'll find it in the "near wilderness" surrounding urban areas.

Prickly lettuce rises with its erect stalk to generally no more than 3 feet. The young leaves are lanceolate with generally rounded ends. They are tender, and if you tear a leaf, you'll see white sap. The plant grows upright with an erect stem, which develops soft spines as it gets older. As the plant matures, you'll note that there is a stiff line of hairs on the bottom midrib of the leaf. The leaf attachment is either sessile or clasping the stem, and the leaf shape can be quite variable, from a simple oblong-lanceolate leaf to one that is divided into pinnately lobed segments. Despite this, after you've seen a few prickly lettuce plants, you should readily recognize it.

The flowers are small and dandelion-like, pale yellow, with about a dozen ray flowers per head. As with dandelion, these mature into small seeds attached to a little cottony tuft.

USES

Prickly lettuce sounds like something you'd really like in a salad, but in fact, you need to find the very youngest leaves or they get too tough and bitter. Very young leaves (before the plant has sent up its flower stalk) are good added to your salads and sandwiches. The leaves can also be collected and mixed into stir-fries, or added to soups or any sort of stew to which you would add wild greens.

But let's not be fooled by the name "lettuce." Yes, it's botanically a relative of

The stalk of the maturing prickly lettuce plant

This is the reason why we don't eat the older prickly lettuce leaves!

the cultivar you buy in the supermarket, but the leaves become significantly bitter as they age, and the rib on the underside of each older leaf develops stiff spines that makes any similarity to lettuce very distant. This means you'll be using this plant raw only when it's very young, and when it's flowering and mature, you probably won't be using it at all.

Still, it's edible, and it grows everywhere. You should get to know this plant and its relatives, and learn to recognize it early in the growing season.

I've used it when very young in sandwiches, salads, soups, stews, and egg dishes. I've even used the small root when I was experimenting with coffee substitutes. Since prickly lettuce is related to dandelion and sow thistle, I figured it would work well as a coffee substitute, and it does, but there's very little root to this plant.

NIPPLEWORT
Lapsana communis

The nipplewort plant PHOTO BY LOUIS-M. LANDRY

Not all botanists agree on this one, but there are believed to be 9 species of *Lapsana* worldwide, and only this species is found in Oregon.

Use: Entire plant eaten
Range: Found throughout the state
Similarity to toxic species: None
Best time: Spring
Status: Somewhat common
Tools needed: Container for collecting

PROPERTIES

This European annual or biennial is a member of the Sunflower family. The plants begin with a basal rosette of leaves. As the plant matures, each leaf has a large end lobe, a bit pointed, with smaller lobes. Though closely related to sow thistle, the appearance is more of a mustard leaf. The upper surface of each leaf is covered in short, tiny hairs.

The nipplewort leaf PHOTO BY LOUIS-M. LANDRY

The leaf stem is triangular in its cross section, though it is very much like celery where it is attached to the main stem. As the flower stalk develops, the leaves that form on the stalk are smaller and narrower.

Flower buds are formed at the tips of the branching stem, and they are smaller, generally less than ¼ inch long. Yellow dandelion-like flowers develop, with 8 bracts surrounding each bud. There are 5 teeth at the end of each petal, just like every other member of the Chicory Tribe.

The bright yellow nipplewort flower
PHOTO BY LOUIS-M. LANDRY

USES

The leaves are best collected when the plant is young, and steaming or boiling is probably the best way to produce the tastiest and most palatable spinach-like dish. You can add nipplewort to soups, stews, and omelettes, or just have it boiled alone and seasoned to taste.

The leaves can be used in salads and are best if mixed with other greens. When chopped and mixed with other greens, the tiny hairs are not noticeable. But if you try to serve a salad of only nipplewort, you're likely to notice the hairs, just as you would with a salad of wild radish greens.

You're going to use this plant very much in the same way in which you use sow thistle in cooked dishes.

SOW THISTLE
Sonchus oleraceus, et al.

The sow thistle plant in flower

There are about 55 species of *Sonchus* worldwide. Four are found in Oregon, all of which are from Europe and are edible.

Use: Mostly the leaves, raw or cooked; root can be cooked and eaten; flower buds pickled
Range: Most common in urban areas, gardens, and farms, but can be found in most environments
Similarity to toxic species: None
Best time: Spring, though the older leaves of late summer are still useful.
Status: Common
Tools needed: Trowel for digging

PROPERTIES
Though the common sow thistle (*S. oleraceus*) is most commonly used for food, the other three species found in Oregon look very similar and can be used the same way. When you see *S. asper*, the prickly sow thistle, you may conclude that it's too much work to use for a dish of cooked greens because it is covered with soft spines.

A young sow thistle plant

Forager note: Sow thistle is one of our most common wild foods. It is so widespread that it can be found in nearly every environment, even in the cracks of urban sidewalks.

When most people see a flowering common sow thistle for the first time, they think it's a dandelion. Yes, it is related to the dandelion, and yes, the flowers are very similar.

Here is a simple distinction: All dandelion leaves arise directly from the taproot, forming a basal rosette. Sow thistle sends up a much taller stalk, up to 5 feet or so in ideal conditions but usually about 3 feet. The leaves are formed along this more or less erect and branching stalk. The leaves are paler and more tender than the dandelion leaves, and sow thistle leaves are not as jagged on the edges as dandelion. And though the individual dandelion and sow thistle flowers are very similar, dandelion only forms one flower per stalk, whereas sow thistle will form many flowers per stalk.

A tender newly emerging sow thistle plant

USES

This was one of the very first wild foods that I learned to identify and eat. It's very common—one of those plants that seems to grow everywhere.

Though sow thistle may not be quite as nutritious as dandelion, it's definitely tastier and the leaves are more tender. You can include the leaves of sow thistle in salads, and even when the plant is old, there is only a hint of bitterness. The flavor and texture are very much like lettuce that you might grow in your garden.

The leaves and tender stems are also ideally added to soups and stews, or simply cooked up by themselves and served like spinach greens. They are tasty alone, or you can try different seasonings (peppers, butter, cheese) that you enjoy.

The root can be eaten or made into a coffee substitute, as is commonly done with two of its relatives, dandelion and chicory. To eat the roots, gather the young ones and boil till tender. Season as you wish, and serve. The roots could also be washed and added to soups and stews.

For a coffee substitute, gather and wash the roots, then dry thoroughly. Grind them into a coarse meal, roast to a light shade of brown, and then percolate into a caffeine-free beverage. Is it "good"? It's all a matter of personal preference.

DANDELION
Taraxacum officinale

A dandelion rosette in flower

There are about 60 species of *Taraxacum* worldwide, with at least 3 of these found in Oregon.

Use: Leaves raw or cooked; root cooked or processed into a beverage
Range: Prefers lawns and fields, and disturbed soils
Similarity to toxic species: None
Best time: Spring for the greens; anytime for the roots
Status: Common
Tools needed: Trowel for the roots

PROPERTIES

Even people who say they don't know how to identify any plants can probably identify a dandelion in a field. The characteristic yellow composite flower sits atop the narrow stem, which arises directly from the taproot. There is one yellow flower per flower stalk. These mature into the round, puffy seed heads that children like to blow on and make a wish.

A young dandelion rosette

Dandelions grow in fields, lawns, vacant lots, and along trails. They tend to prefer disturbed soils, though I have seen them in the wilderness.

The leaves are dark green, toothed on the margins, and each arises from the root. The name "dandelion" actually comes from the French *dent de leon*, meaning "tooth of the lion," for the jagged edges of the leaves.

USES

My first exposure to dandelion was at about age 7, when my father would pay me a nickel to dig them out of our front yard lawn and throw them into the trash. Boy, things have changed! These days, I would not consider having a front lawn, and I definitely would not dig out the dandelions and toss them in the trash.

Dandelion is another versatile wild food. It's not native to Oregon but is now found all over the world. The yellow flowers make the plant conspicuous in fields and lawns, though it's really the leaves and root that are most used by the forager.

If you want raw dandelion greens, you'll want to pick them as early as possible in the season, or they become bitter. The bitterness is not bad, and it can be mellowed out by adding other greens. Also, oil-rich dressing makes a dandelion salad more palatable.

It's understandable that dandelions have gotten more popular—they are,

The dandelion plant going to seed

The washed root of a dandelion plant

after all, the richest source of beta carotene, even more so than carrots. However, not all the greens sold as "dandelion" in farmers' markets and supermarkets are the genuine leaf. Frequently we will see various endive relatives sold and called "dandelion."

Mr. Xiong collects bundles of dandelion greens from his farm and sells them at farmers' markets.

The roots are also edible. The younger roots, and plants growing in rich soil, are more tender and more desirable. But I have eaten old roots and tough roots and have found a way to make them palatable. Generally, I scrub the roots to get rid of all the soil, and then boil until tender. You can boil them whole or slice them and, when tender, use in stews and soups.

For a "coffee-substitute" beverage, wash and then dry the roots. Though there are a few ways you can do this, I generally do a coarse grind and then roast them in the oven until they are mildly brown. Then I do a fine grind and percolate them into a beverage. You can drink it "black" or add honey and cream.

BARBERRY FAMILY (BERBERIDACEAE)

The Barberry family consists of about 16 genera and approximately 670 species worldwide. Only 3 of these genera are found in Oregon.

OREGON GRAPE (a.k.a. BARBERRY)
Berberis aquifolium

The mature fruit and leaves of the Oregon grape bush

The fruits of all members of the *Berberis* genus are edible. In Oregon you'll find common Oregon grape (*B. aquifolium*), mountain Oregon grape (*B. nervosa*), and 7 other species.

Use: Fruits eaten raw or made into wine, jams, or jellies
Range: Most common in the Cascades and in the western part of Oregon in coniferous forests, slopes, canyons, woodlands, and thickets. Often used as an ornamental.
Similarity to toxic species: None
Best time: Summer
Status: Common
Tools needed: Berry-collecting basket

PROPERTIES
This is a low-growing to medium-size shrub, though some are low-growing and spreading. Leaves are alternately arranged and pinnately compound. The leaflets are holly-like with spines along their margins. Flowers are yellow and are formed in racemes. The sepals and the petals are similar, usually in 5 whorls. The

Some flowers of the Oregon grape

A view of the fruit of the Oregon grape and the pinnately-divided leaf

approximately ¼-inch fruits are bluish to purple berries and are tightly arranged in clusters that resemble tiny grapes. However, this plant is not botanically related to the true grapes (*Vitis* spp.).

Though Oregon grape can be found throughout the state, it is most common in the west in wooded areas. It is also planted as an ornamental, so it will be found outside of its native terrain.

USES

My experience with the Oregon grape is mostly as a trail nibble, and on occasion I have had a least a handful to mash and use as a pancake topping. These small oval berries are tart and refreshing, high in vitamin C, and make a good jelly when sweetened.

According to Cecilia Garcia and Dr. James Adams in *Healing with Medicinal Plants of the West*, the fruits of all the members of the *Berberis* genus, generally all commonly called "Oregon grape," were eaten raw or cooked by most Indians wherever the plant grew. *B. nervosa*'s blue to purplish fruits were gathered by the Yana people from the foothills and dried, then ground into a flour that was used

An Oregon grape that has been planted in an urban yard as an edible ornamental

for a mush. Many of the indigenous people made drinks from these fruits. They are also quite good dried and used as a snack food or added to cookies, cakes, or other dishes as you'd add raisins.

Garcia and Adams noted that the fruit also has antihistamine activity, which may relieve indigestion. And according to Paul Campbell, author of *Earth Pigments and Paint of the California Indians*, the fruits are especially useful in making traditional blue pigment and paint.

BIRCH FAMILY (BETULACEAE)

The Birch family consists of 6 genera and about 155 species worldwide. Three of these genera are found in Oregon.

HAZELNUT (a.k.a. BEAKED HAZELNUT)
Corylus cornuta

A view of the leaf and fruit of the hazelnut PHOTO BY KEIR MORSE

The *Corylus* genus has about 15 species worldwide, with only 2 found in Oregon.

Use: Edible nuts
Range: Found on the edges of forests, slopes, and many other habitats throughout Oregon; prefers shady environments
Similarity to toxic species: None
Best time: Late summer into fall, when nuts mature
Status: Common
Tools needed: Bag or box for collecting

A view of the leaf and fruit of the hazelnut PHOTO BY KEIR MORSE

PROPERTIES

This large shrub, or small tree, can grow up to 25 feet tall and can easily be confused for an alder. The leaves are oval to round, alternate, with a rounded base and pointed tip. The whole leaf is about 3 inches long, with double-toothed margins. The leaves are more or less hairy (really, more like a fine fuzz) on both sides.

The nuts, which mature from September through October, are formed in pairs. A papery, bristly outer husk covers the nut, which has a thin, brittle inner shell. When you see the exposed nut, it will remind you of a commercial filbert, to which it's related. It's relatively easy to identify this tree when you find it, and it's easy to harvest the nuts.

USES

This is an excellent nut, and you'd use it in any of the ways in which you'd use a filbert: raw, roasted, slivered, etc. This means you can shell them and eat them raw in nut mixes, in salads, and even sprinkled into bread or pancake batter. Try sprinkling them on ice cream. The nuts can also be ground into a meal and used to form cakes or added to other pastry dough.

Nuts are one of the great survival foods since they have the oils necessary for life. They store a long time, provide some quick energy with no cooking, and give our bodies a lot of what they need.

BORAGE (OR WATERLEAF) FAMILY (BORAGINACEAE)

The Borage family consists of 120 genera and about 2,300 species worldwide. At least 22 of these genera are found in Oregon.

MOUNTAIN BLUEBELLS
Mertensia ciliata

A view of the mountain bluebells in flower PHOTO BY JEAN PAWEK

There are about 50 species worldwide, with at least 7 in Oregon.

Use: Edible
Range: Generally found in the mountains, along stream banks
Similarity to toxic species: None
Best time: Spring
Status: Somewhat common within its range
Tools needed: Container for collecting

PROPERTIES
This plant will grow in the dry sagebrush country of eastern Oregon, though generally it is a mountain plant, found along streams and in meadows. Its most common range is from the foothills to the subalpine.

Mountain bluebells, also known as streamside bluebells, begin with many stems at a woody base, growing up to 4 feet tall with large clusters of stems and many flowers. The basal leaves are elliptical in shape, with a long petiole. The leaves that develop on the stems are smaller, still elliptical, and are nearly stemless (sessile).

The blue flowers are formed in branched, hanging clusters, with petals approximately ½ inch long, and nearly united so that the flowers appear tubular. The styles (the stalk-like part of the pistil) extend slightly beyond the petals. The overall appearance is of hanging bells, hence the name.

The leaves and flowers of mountain bluebell

In general, all the species of *Mertensia* can be used for food, and all are generally called bluebells. Sometimes these are referred to as "chiming bells" to differentiate them from the many other unrelated plants that are often also called "bluebells." There are perhaps 7 to 9 species of *Mertensia* in this area. The tall species that grow from 1 to 4 feet tall and found in moist habitats are *M. ciliata* and *M. paniculata*. Shorter species, smaller than a foot, are found at the higher and drier subalpine to alpine areas. These include *M. oblongifolia*, *M. longiflora*, *M. bella*, and *M. perplexa*.

USES

The tender leaves can be used as a hiking snack. According to some, they have a slight oyster-like flavor.

In its zone this is one of the best green plants that you can find. The leaves, tender stems, and flowers can all be used raw for salad when the entire plant is still succulent, or you can just trim off the young tips and stir-fry, steam, or sauté them. You could even add some fresh leaves to a sandwich.

Older plants can get a little hairy, though this doesn't detract from palatability. Still, older leaves are best cooked.

CAUTIONS

This plant is considered toxic if you consume it in "large" quantities, due to the presence of various alkaloids. We've not heard of any recorded cases of toxicity, however.

MUSTARD FAMILY (BRASSICACEAE)

The Mustard family is another large family, comprising more than 330 genera worldwide and about 3,780 species. This large family is subdivided into 8 groups. In Oregon the Mustard family is represented by at least 56 genera.

The floral characteristics that define the Mustard family are that it has 4 free petals, 4 sepals (generally white or yellow, but other colors as well), 6 stamens (4 long, 2 short), 1 pistil, a superior ovary, and fruits generally a capsule or silique with 2 valves. Many are cultivated for foods and some for ornamentals. Botanists divide this family into 8 groups. Dr. Leonid Enari stated that he was unaware of any toxic member of this entire family, though some are more palatable than others. As a result, I have experimented with many of the Mustard family species in various parts of North America. The most common edible members are presented here.

The typical leaf shape for this family is lyrately pinnate, meaning a large terminal lobe and smaller lateral lobes. Once I asked a fellow botanist for help in identifying the genus of a plant I'd found, which I knew was in the Mustard family. He replied, "Trying to identify a *Brassicaceae* when not in flower is not exactly fun." Well said! These are much easier to identify once they have flowered.

WINTERCRESS
Barbarea vulgaris and *B. verna*

The rosette of the wintercress plant

There are approximately 22 species of *Barbarea* worldwide, and 3 are found in Oregon.

Use: Leaves are eaten.
Range: Common in disturbed soils, fields, and along roads
Similarity to toxic species: None
Best time: Spring
Status: Found widely throughout the state, common in areas
Tools needed: Collecting bag

PROPERTIES

When you see wintercress for the first time, you will notice the obvious resemblance to watercress. Of course, they are both in the Mustard family, and both have the same lyrately pinnate leaves so typical of many members of this family.

The lyrately pinnate leaves of wintercress

Wintercress leaves have the same shade of green that you see in watercress. However, watercress is found only in the water or at the edges of slow-moving streams. Wintercress is found anywhere, and usually *not* in the water. It grows in the soil, usually disturbed. It can be near the water, but it can also be far from water. It would not be uncommon to find wintercress in a roadside ditch where water collects.

It's called wintercress because it has the ability to live through the winter, to overwinter, when most other plants die from the frost.

The leaves tend to form a rosette, and it doesn't sprawl like watercress. One of the key differences is that watercress has white flowers and wintercress has yellow flowers. The flower structure of wintercress is like that of all members of this family: 4 petals, 4 sepals, 6 stamens (2 short, 4 tall), and 1 pistil.

USES

Taste a bit of the wintercress. You'll find it a bit bitter, even when young. The leaf is not strongly bitter, but it's bitter nevertheless. For this reason, you'll probably not use these leaves as an exclusive salad ingredient. They can be mixed with other ingredients for salad, with an oil dressing to help mellow the bitterness. Of course, everyone is different, and if you like this flavor, by all means enjoy it abundantly in your salads.

Wintercress in flower PHOTO BY BARBARA KOLANDER

In my experience wintercress is better as a cooked green, either boiled or steamed, in soups, stews, egg dishes, etc. The tender tops of the plants (leaves and immature flowers) can be boiled or steamed and served with butter, cheese, or other cooked vegetables.

As with every wild food, I always recommend trying this by itself so you get to know the plant's characteristics. Then, you'll probably see why the plant is usually cooked and typically blended with other foods to offset the bitterness.

According to the Live Gourmet company, which hydroponically grows *Barbarea verna*, with roots attached, for sale in supermarkets under the trade name of "upland cress," *B. verna* is "high in phytonutrients, antioxidants and vitamins . . . with as much vitamin C as an orange, more calcium than milk, high levels of magnesium, lutein, phosphorus, potassium, iron, beta-carotene, vitamins A, B1, B6, K, rich fiber, and zero fat."

MUSTARD
Brassica spp.

A young black mustard plant

There are 35 species worldwide, and at least 6 are found in Oregon.

Use: Leaves raw or cooked, seeds for spice, flowers for garnish
Range: Fields, urban areas, and chaparral hillsides
Similarity to toxic species: None
Best time: Spring for greens and flowers
Status: Widespread
Tools needed: None

PROPERTIES
Though you should learn to recognize the common mustards even when the plant is not in flower, it is the flower that will initially draw you to the plant. The bright-yellow flower has the typical Mustard family flora arrangement: 4 petals (shaped in an X or cross), 4 sepals (1 under each petal), 6 stamens (4 long, 2 short), and 1 pistil. These are formed in a raceme with the buds toward the tops, then the mature flowers, and then, lower on the stalk, the seedpods forming. The seedpods are about an inch long and needle thin.

A view of the leaves and stalks of one of the mustards

The initial basal leaves are lyrately pinnately divided, meaning that they have the appearance of a guitar with a large round lateral lobe and smaller side lobes. Not exactly like a guitar, but that gives you a good mental picture. As the plant matures, the leaves that form on the upper stalks are smaller and linear and look nothing like the young basal leaves.

USES

Mustard is one of the first wild foods that I began to eat, partly because it is so common, and partly because it is so easy to identify. I recall seeing a line drawing of it in Bradford Angier's book *Free for the Eating*, which didn't look anything like the green plant with yellow flowers that I was seeing everywhere. Angier used a picture of the mature plant gone to seed, and I was seeing the young spring plant. They were both right, but it demonstrated to me the need to always learn plants by observing them in the field, and observing them throughout their entire growing season.

I began with the young mustard greens, chewing the raw leaves and enjoying the spicy flavor, despite the fine hairs covering the leaves (not all *Brassica* are hairy). I then moved on to chopping them up and adding them to salads, which was good. I then began to boil the leaves and serve them to my family, with butter. Everyone enjoyed them, even my father. Eventually I found that I could add mustard greens to just about any dish: soups, mixed salads, omelettes, stir-fries, potatoes, you name it!

Forager note: This is a hardy plant. I have managed to find some mustard greens even during droughts when no other greens were available.

The young mustard rosette

Mustard flowers

The flower buds and flowers have also been a good trail treat and make a good colorful garnish to salads and soups. I give them to children and tell them that they taste like broccoli, and most of the children say they enjoy the flowers.

Naturalist Barbara Kolander collects mustard flowers.

The tender tops of the stems with the flower buds can also be snapped off the upper part of the plant, steamed, and served with some sauce or cheese. The flavor is just like the Chinese broccoli that you buy at farmers' markets.

Lastly, you can come back to this annual plant in late fall, when the leaves are dried up and the tops are just tan-colored stems with small seedpods. Collect the pods in a bag, and break them up. The seeds go to the bottom of the bag, and you can discard the pod shells. The brown seeds are then used as a seasoning for various dishes calling for mustard, or you can try making your own mustard from them.

RECIPE

Pascal's Mustard

Fellow forager Pascal Baudar takes the pungent flowers of regular black mustard and grinds them while fresh, adding white wine and vinegar to taste. He thus produces a mustard condiment from the flowers, not the seeds as is the usual custom. This makes a delicious mustard with a new twist.

SEA ROCKET
Cakile edentula and C. maritima

The sea rocket plant growing in the sand at the Pacific Ocean

There are 7 species of *Cakile* worldwide, and these 2 are found in Oregon. Sea rocket is found on the beach shores of North America, Africa, and Europe. On Oregon's west coast, we have *C. edentula* (American sea rocket) and *C. maritime* (European sea rocket), both introduced.

Use: Greens, sprouts, and flowers are edible, ideally cooked, but can be used raw sparingly.
Range: Restricted to the sandy beaches along the entire coast
Similarity to toxic species: None
Best time: Spring, but can be picked year-round
Status: Somewhat common
Tools needed: None

PROPERTIES
Sea rocket is widespread along the Oregon coast, growing in the sand in the upper areas of the beach, usually just beyond the high-tide line in the dunes. When you see how well these plants have naturalized, it is hard to believe that

The sea rocket plant sprawling on the beach

they are not natives. *C. maritime* is the one that you see most commonly on the beaches, and it is native to Europe. *C. edentula* is also found and is native to the east coast of the United States.

The leaves are very much like a small mustard leaf but plump, as if the mustard leaf were swollen. Each leaf has a bluish-green appearance, with the leaves pinnately divided into linear segments. Typically, each leaf tends to fold inward along the central vein of the leaf. The seedpods also look swollen, and you can see why the plant is called "rocket" by looking at the pod's space-rocket appearance.

Of course, the lavender to light-purple flower has the typical mustard flower arrangement of 4 petals, 4 sepals, 6 stamens, and 1 pistil.

USES

The leaves are strongly flavored like horseradish, and generally you would not want to include the mature leaves in a salad. But boiling tones them down quite a bit, and they are then tastier and more palatable. The boiled leaves can be added to flavor soup broths or to dishes of mixed greens. In general, you'd probably not

The individual sea rocket leaf PHOTO BY RICK ADAMS   Sea rocket seedpods and flowers PHOTO BY RICK ADAMS

want to serve them alone as a cooked green unless you changed the water once and then served them with some onions and probably a savory sauce.

Still, they can turn an otherwise bland meal into quite a treat. They will help to flavor clam chowder and other soups and stews, and will really liven up stale old MREs.

Sometimes, if you're at the beach during late winter, you might find an old sea rocket plant whose seeds have all dropped into the sand and sprouted. You can carefully harvest dozens of these strongly flavored sprouts and add them to your soup or salad.

Think of sea rocket more as a flavoring agent and garnish, and not as a principal food.

RECIPE

Ocean Side Wasabi

Finely dice sea rocket leaves into nearly a paste, then add a very small amount of oil and vinegar and mix to create a passable "wasabi."

BITTERCRESS
Cardamine spp.

The plant growing in a pot

A closeup of bittercress

There are about 200 species of *Cardamine* worldwide, and 15 can be found in Oregon, all edible. The most common seem to be *C. hirsuta* and *C. oligosperma*.

Use: Leaves and all tender portions can be eaten.
Range: Common in the western United States, including parts of Oregon
Similarity to toxic species: None
Best time: Spring
Status: Widespread in localized areas
Tools needed: None

PROPERTIES
Bittercress can be very common in certain areas, mostly in gardens, where it appears as a common weed. The plant prefers moist and disturbed soils. It grows from sea level up to the foothills.

The small plant begins with a somewhat orderly appearing rosette of pinnately divided basal leaves. Each leaflet is generally round, all about the same size, though the terminal lobe is slightly larger—which is the case in just about all members of the Mustard family, except these leaves are very small. Each leaf can be about 2 inches long, with the terminal lobe about ½ inch wide.

One or more flower stalks may arise from the root. As the flower stalk arises, the leaves appearing on the stalk are similar, though the leaflets become more linear.

The bright-white flowers appear mostly in the early spring and the early fall, though you can find the plant in flower nearly year-round. The flower pattern, like all members of the Mustard family, is 4 petals, 4 sepals, 6 stamens, and 1 pistil. The seedpods that follow the flowers are thin, like little needles, and about an inch long, more or less.

Though somewhat short-lived, the plant can be collected anytime in its growing season. The little seedpods of this plant are known to pop open, throwing the seeds, which is why the plant can be found so abundantly within local areas.

USES

If you have a garden, you've probably pulled *C. oligosperma* or *C. hirsute* out of your pots and garden space, whether you knew its name or not. It's a small plant, it's an annual, and it spreads and spreads. Gardeners seem to hate it, even though they could eat it. Most gardeners and nurserymen that I've talked to regard this as a serious nuisance plant, along with oxalis. At least one person questioned why I would even consider including a plant such as this in a book of edible wild plants. "Because it's edible!" I replied. But I do understand that sentiment—I've seen areas that were nearly covered with a sea of bittercress.

The leaves are good raw when very young and can be added to salads, soups, and various cooked dishes. They become just a bit stronger and bitter as they mature. In fact, any tender part of the plant can be added to a salad, soup, stew, or other cooked dish. The older leaves are edible too. They can have a stronger flavor, but cooking mellows them and makes them more palatable.

You would not want to make a whole meal from this plant, partly because the leaves are so tiny that it takes a bit of time to gather a reasonable amount, and then it cooks down to very little bulk. But if you have this plant in abundance, you shouldn't overlook it. It's a nutritious, tasty addition to many dishes, as well as sandwiches. Consider it more of a garnish or spice when you add it your meals. When in season and abundant, it's easy to collect several handfuls. Rinse them to get rid of dirt, and add to your salad for a spicy addition.

I also find bittercress tasty when cooked like spinach, though it is a bit of work to collect enough for one pot of greens.

SHEPHERD'S PURSE
Capsella bursa-pastoris

The young leaves of shepherd's purse

There are 4 species of *Capsella* worldwide, and only this one is found in Oregon.

Use: Leaves eaten raw or cooked; medicine
Range: Prefers lawns, fields, and disturbed soils
Similarity to toxic species: None
Best time: Spring is best for greens; the seeds can be collected late spring to early summer.
Status: Somewhat common
Tools needed: None

PROPERTIES
Shepherd's purse is most easily identified by its flat, heart-shaped seedpods. They are unmistakable! The stalks rise about a foot or so tall. The little clusters of four-petalled white flowers, sometimes tinged with a bit of purple, are formed in racemes along the stalk. These then mature into the heart-shaped pods. Trouble is, by the time you see all the seedpods, it's usually too late to use the young leaves for food, but now you know how to recognize shepherd's purse for the next season.

A young rosette of shepherd's purse with the emerging flower stalk. Note the heart-shaped seedpod.

A view of the shepherd's purse seed stalk, with the heart-shaped seedpods, arising from a bed of chickweed.

The young leaves are often hidden in the grass, making them somewhat inconspicuous. The basal leaves are toothed, with a large terminal lobe, typical of Mustard family leaves. The upper leaves are without a stalk and are more arrowhead shaped. If you look closely, the young leaves will be covered with little hairs.

USES

The flavor of shepherd's purse leaves is mild, and they could be used in just about any recipe calling for tender greens, such as salads, sandwiches, soups, tostados, eggs, etc. However, they seem to be best when used in salads.

Additionally, once it was well established in North America, some Native Americans ground the seeds into a meal and used it in drinks and as a flour for various dishes.

Dr. Leonid Enari used to poll his students on which plant tasted the best of the many wild plants he let them try. Consistently in his polls, shepherd's purse was rated the best. It is actually somewhat bland and peppery, but not too peppery, and the texture is mild. Even finicky eaters will like these leaves.

It's also very nutritious. About ½ cup of the leaves (100 g) contains 208 mg of calcium, 86 mg of phosphorus, 40 mg of sodium, 394 mg of potassium, 36 mg of vitamin C, and 1,554 IU of vitamin A.

Dr. Enari told his students that this was the best plant to stop a nosebleed. You boil the plant, dip a cotton ball into the water, and then apply to the nose. It turns out that many people have used this plant medicinally, especially to stop internal or external bleeding.

WATERCRESS
Nasturtium officinale

A view of watercress along the edge of a stream

There are 5 species of *Nasturtium* worldwide, with at least 2 found in Oregon.

Use: Leaves eaten raw or cooked in salads, stir-fries, soup, etc.; can be dried for use as seasoning
Range: Restricted to the edges of lakes and streams
Similarity to toxic species: None
Best time: Summer, before the plant flowers; however, the plant can be collected anytime.
Status: Somewhat common along streams
Tools needed: None

PROPERTIES
Once you learn to recognize watercress and see how the pinnately divided leaves are formed, you will find it quite easy to recognize, whether it is very young or older and flowering. First, it nearly always grows directly on the edges of streams where the water is slower. Occasionally you'll find it in sandy areas, but it is always in an area that is at least seasonally underwater. You'll typically find it growing in thick mats.

The leaves are pinnately divided into round leaflets. The stems are hollow, and there are white hairs on the underwater part of the stem. The plant is in the Mustard family, so when it gets older and flowers, the white flowers will be divided into the typical Mustard formula: 4 petals, 4 sepals, 6 stamens, and 1 pistil.

A view of watercress in the wild

Though watercress can today be found worldwide, it is regarded by botanists as a native plant. It was known to be a part of the diet of early Native Americans.

EDIBILITY

Watercress was one of the very first wild plants that I learned how to identify and began to use. It is not only common throughout waterways in Oregon but throughout the world.

I have always enjoyed making a salad of mixed greens, including watercress. But I don't usually make a salad with only watercress because it's a bit too spicy for my taste. A few raw watercress leaves are also tasty in sandwiches.

Watercress makes a delicious soup. Just finely chop the entire plant (tender stems and leaves) and add it to a water- or milk-based soup. Or you can add chopped watercress leaves to a miso base.

You can also cook the greens like spinach, serving it with a simple seasoning such as butter or cheese. Or try mixing the greens into an egg omelette. If you're living off MREs or freeze-dried camping food, you can add some diced watercress to liven up your meals.

Also, for those of you who like making your own spices, you can dry and powder watercress and use it to season various dishes. Use it alone, or blend the powdered watercress with powdered seaweed or other flavorful herbs. You'll notice that some of the commercial salt-alternative spices use dried watercress leaves.

Another self-reliance idea is to dry wild foods into the basis of a soup stock, and then reconstitute later into a soup or stew broth. Dried and powdered watercress makes an ideal ingredient in such a mix.

Watercress in flower, with four-petalled white flowers PHOTO BY HELEN WONG

MEDICINAL USES

Watercress has numerous medicinal applications. Some of the most popular, and most documented, include eating watercress to prevent eczema from returning or for inflammatory flare-ups, as well as using an extract of watercress (obtained by boiling the leaves for 10 minutes in water) as a disinfectant to wash the eczema area.

RECIPE

Saturday Night Special

Gently sauté half an onion bulb, diced, in a skillet with butter. You could substitute a handful of wild or garden onion greens. Quickly add at least 1 cup of watercress, chopped into large pieces, and cook gently until all is tender. Add a dash of soy sauce and serve.

As a tea, watercress acts as a digestive aid, as the mustard oil glycosides, vitamins, and bitters in the tea promote production of the stomach juices that aid digestion. With its high potassium content, watercress tea assists the kidneys by acting as a diuretic, cleansing the urinary tract. Because watercress contains high levels of lutein, an essential antioxidant for eye health, eating it is good for your eyes. Consuming watercress, or drinking a tea from the leaves, is also helpful with respiratory problems, due to its expectorant qualities and magnesium content.

In fact, you get all these benefits, more or less, by consuming any member of the Mustard family, though watercress and wintercress have been studied the most. (Source for medicinal aspects: www.LiveGourmet.com.)

CAUTIONS

If you have doubts about the purity of the water where you get your watercress, you should not eat it raw; boil it first and then use it in a cooked dish. Always wash the watercress before using it. It grows right in the water, and you want to remove any dirt or other undesirables that may be clinging to the plant.

WILD RADISH
Raphanus sativus and *R. raphanistrum*

The flowers of wild radish are typically lavender, with some white, and more rarely pale yellow.

There are 3 species of *Raphanus* worldwide. These 2 are found in Oregon, both native to the Mediterranean. The latter is also referred to as "jointed charlock."

Use: All tender portions of this plant—leaf, stems, pods, flowers—can be eaten raw, pickled, or cooked. Roots generally are not used.

Range: Fields, wet areas, farmlands, vacant lots, and disturbed soils

Similarity to toxic species: None

Best time: Spring into summer

Status: Common

Tools needed: Clippers

PROPERTIES

Each young leaf of the wild radish is lyrately pinnately divided, meaning that there is one large end lobe and smaller side lobes or segments to the leaf. It resembles a guitar! When the young leaves of wild radish are newly emerging, it would be easy to confuse the leaves with those of mustard (*Brassica* spp.). However, wild radish leaves lack the fine hairs that you find on mustard. If you examine a wild radish leaf closely, it will be covered somewhat sparsely with bristles, but the leaf is smoother (than mustard) and you will see a tinge of red in the midrib of the radish leaf.

The seedpods of the wild radish

Another view of the young wild radish leaves

The young leaves of the wild radish plant

Wild radish roots are typically thin and less robust than the two pictured here.

As the plant flowers, instead of the usual yellow mustard flowers, the flowers will be lavender or white, or very rarely a pale yellow. There is the typical Mustard family flower formula of 4 petals, 4 sepals, 6 stamens (4 long and 2 short), and 1 pistil. The flowers are followed by fleshy seedpods that resemble pointed jalapeño peppers.

The root of wild radish is a white taproot, not at all like the radish you might grow in your garden or buy at the store. It is largely woody and inedible, though there is a soft outer layer that can be peeled off. The taste of this outer root layer is so obviously "radish" that most anyone can identify this plant by that aroma and flavor.

Overall, wild radish can grow up to 4 feet, even taller in ideal conditions.

USES

The wild radish has many edible parts. The leaves can be collected at any time in their growing cycle, cut into small pieces, and added to salads. They are hot and spicy, so add to other greens. The leaves can also be added to soups, stews, and egg dishes.

The flowers are quite tasty and sweet when you first pick and nibble them, but your mouth will get very hot. Eat them sparingly. You can pick the flowers and add them to salads and other dishes as a tasty garnish. The tender flower tips—somewhat resembling Chinese broccoli—can be snapped free, steamed or boiled, and served with butter, cheese, or a spicy sauce.

The green seedpods, which somewhat resemble jalapeño or serrano chilies, can be nibbled when they are still tender inside and haven't gotten woody. You can add the chopped tender pods to soups and salads, or try pickling them.

RECIPE

Pickled Radish Pods

Pickled radish pods were very popular in the Victorian era. It's a neat way to preserve them, and they're wonderful in salads, sandwiches, or side dishes. They are also very easy to make.

For this recipe, we use ½-pint jars. Simply fill up the jar with as much (clean) radish pods as you can, and in each jar place the following:

2 garlic cloves

½ teaspoon Italian or French spice mix (or dill or other spice of your liking)

1 medium spicy dehydrated chili (just because I like some heat)

⅓ Oregon myrtle leaf (or regular bay leaf)

½ teaspoon sea salt

In a saucepan, make a pickling solution composed of 3 parts apple cider vinegar and 2 parts white wine. Bring the solution to a boil and pour it into the jars. Close the lids and place the jars in the fridge. Wait 2–3 weeks before consuming.

If you know how to can and want to preserve the pods outside the fridge (shelf stable), use the water bath method and boil for 15 minutes.

—RECIPE FROM PASCAL BAUDAR

HEDGE MUSTARD
Sisymbrium spp.

A view of the *Sisymbrium* rosette

There are 41 species of *Sisymbrium* worldwide, with 5 found in Oregon, all native to Europe.

Use: Leaves, raw or cooked
Range: Prefers disturbed soils of fields and farms, or along roadsides and trails
Similarity to toxic species: None
Best time: Spring
Status: Common
Tools needed: None

PROPERTIES
If you already know the mustards (*Brassica* spp.), you will very likely think "mustard" when you see a hedge mustard. The flowers of *Sisymbrium* tend to be smaller than the *Brassica* flowers, and the leaves tend to be more pointy compared to the rounder leaves of *Brassica*. Of course, to botanists, the distinction is mostly in the details of the flowers, but with sufficient observation, you'll be able to recognize the hedge mustards by leaf alone.

Note the unique configuration of the *Sisymbrium* leaves.

A view of *Sisymbrium irio* in flower

Someone underground likes this *Sisymbrium.*

USES

I think of the *Sisymbriums* as wild wasabi. Chew on a bit of the leaf, and you'll get that hot horseradishy effect that opens your nostrils. I have friends who actually turn these leaves into a wild wasabi, which is great on sandwiches and crackers or as a dip. But generally, I regard the hedge mustards as a source of very spicy greens that go well with salads, soups, egg dishes, sandwiches, stir-fries—just about any dish where you can add greens. These are spicy greens, in general a bit spicier than the greens of the common mustards (*Brassicas*).

I have had broths made from the finely diced hedge mustard leaves, into which a lot of rice had been added. This dish was hot and good! I have also had "wild kimchee" that consisted of wild greens that had been marinated in raw apple cider vinegar. A lot of hedge mustard leaves were used in one of these kimchees, and it was delicious. You could also dry the hedge mustard leaves and either reconstitute later, or just powder them and use as a seasoning.

The flowers are good too, but they aren't quite as good as the *Brassica* mustard flowers. Hedge mustard flowers seem to have too much of that bitter and astringent bite, so I use them sparingly in soups, salads, or other dishes.

RECIPE

Screaming at the Moon

A hedge mustard soup recipe.

2 cups chopped hedge mustard greens

2 garlic cloves, peeled and crushed

3 cups water

¼ cup miso powder

Simmer the greens and garlic with the water in a covered pot. When tender, add the miso and cook another 5 minutes. Serves 2–3.

CACTUS FAMILY (CACTACEAE)

There are 125 genera in the Cactus family and about 1,800 species worldwide, mostly in the American deserts. Three genera are found in Oregon.

According to Dr. Leonid Enari, the entire Cactus family is a very safe family for consumption. However, he would quickly add that some are much too woody for food. A very few are extremely bitter—even after boiling—and you would not even consider using them for food.

If you choose to experiment, just remember that palatability is the key. Don't eat any that are too woody or any that are extremely bitter. Any plants that have a white sap when cut are not cacti but look-alike members of the *Euphorbia* group. Nearly all species of *Opuntia* have a long history of being used for food.

PRICKLY PEAR
Opuntia spp.

Wild prickly pear pads

At least 3 species of *Opuntia* are found in the wild in Oregon. These are generally called prickly pear cacti or cholla cacti.

Use: Young pads for food, raw or cooked; fruits for desserts and juices; seeds for flour
Range: Eastern Oregon in the Columbia Plateau area and the southeast up into the Harney Lake area and the Great Basin influence. *Opuntia fragilis* (yellow flowers) can thrive beneath a blanket of snow.
Similarity to toxic species: See Cautions

Best time: Spring is best to collect the new pads, though the older ones can also be used. September through October is best for harvesting the fruits.
Status: Common locally
Tools needed: Metal tongs, sturdy bucket, possibly gloves

PROPERTIES

Prickly pear cacti are readily recognized by their flat to oval pads, with their spines evenly spaced over the surface. The cacti flower by summer, and then the fruits mature by September and October.

The key to using this plant is to find a way to harvest and clean it without getting the spines—and the finer hairlike glochids at the base of each spine—in your fingers. The pads are generally easier to harvest than the fruits, though I still recommend using metal tongs with each. The very young, still glossy-green pads can be scraped with a sharp knife to remove the spines and glochids, then rinsed before using in a recipe.

Another way to remove the spines and glochids is to hold the pad with metal tongs and singe the pad over a flame for a few seconds.

The fruits tend to have more glochids, so I always collect those with metal tongs. Still using the tongs, I turn each fruit over in a flame—about 10 seconds—to burn off the spines and glochids. Then I cut them in half, remove the fruit inside, and eat, preserve, or process them in some way.

USES

There are better cacti for eating than the species found in Oregon, but if you're stuck in the high plains of eastern Oregon, a prickly pear might compose a part of your meal. And there are several ways to get a meal from the prickly pear cactus: young pad, old pad, fruit, seed.

Whether you pick your pads from the wild or grow them in your backyard, the new growth of spring offers one of the more readily available foods, with the least amount of work. Remember, the cacti all have some spines and the tiny little glochids, so you'll need to be careful whether you work with the very young or the very old pads. Some varieties are less spiny than others—those are the ones I choose.

Forager note: If you collect cacti, you will—sooner or later—get spines and glochids in your skin. Spines are easy to see and relatively easy to remove, but glochids are smaller and hairlike and more difficult to remove from the skin. Try smearing white glue on the part of your body that has glochids. Let the glue dry, then peel it off. This will usually remove most glochids.

When you get the very young pads of spring, they are still bright green and the tough outer layer won't yet have developed. Carefully pick them, and then you can quickly burn off the young spines or thoroughly scrape each side to remove all spines and glochids. Then you can slice or dice the pads, and first sauté to remove much of their liquid and sliminess. Cook off the water, and then add eggs, potatoes, or even tofu for a delicious stew.

Older pads are also edible, but their flavor and texture is different. If you simply cut a large prickly pear pad in half, you'll see that the fiber is all toward the surface. You can carefully slice off the outer fiber layer and use the insides. (This will work most of the time, but in times of drought, the pads can be so shriveled that there's not much to actually eat.)

The flavor and texture resembles squash, and you can use these older cactus pads in soups or stews, or the more traditional manner of cooking with eggs.

The fruits are delicious too, and they are the closest thing to watermelon that you'll find in the wild, aside from the abundance of tiny seeds. If I am out on a walk and just see a few ripe fruits, I will carefully pick the fruit, scrape off the stickers with my pocketknife, slice the fruit in half, and lift out the inner edible portion.

Prickly pear fruits ("tunas") and pads ("nopales")

These prickly pear pads have been cleaned of their spines and glochids and sliced in preparation for a cooked dish.

However, when I intentionally go out to harvest fruit, I go with a plastic tub and metal salad tongs and carefully fill the tub with the ripe fruit. Then, at home, using the metal tongs, I quickly pass each fruit through a flame to burn off

Monica Montoya tastes some of the raw prickly pear pad.

the glochids and spines, and then rinse and wash them. I cut open each fruit and will eat it as is. Or I will deseed them and store them for later use for drinks, jams, pie filling, etc. I deseed the fruits by putting the cleaned and peeled fruits into a blender. I blend it for a minute or so at a low speed, and then I pour the juice through a metal strainer to remove all the seed.

An excellent drink is made by mixing 50 percent of this cactus fruit puree with 50 percent spring water.

In the old days even the seeds from the prickly pear fruits were saved, dried, and ground into flour. I've tried it a few times. They have a unique flavor, but it's a lot of work.

Eating the prickly pear pads (raw, cooked, in juice) has long been considered a way to combat diabetes. For those who don't want to grow, clean, or cook their own nopales, you can now purchase the powder (or pills), which you consume in various ways in order to combat diabetes. But consider this: If you have diabetes and you try to change your habits and diet to cure yourself, and you start to eat cactus but there is no change in your diabetic condition, the worst that has happened is that you have been eating cactus. With some of the diabetic medicines that have been introduced in recent decades, thousands of people have died from the very drug that was intended to cure! Oops. Sometimes it's really worthwhile to look to the past for a more fulfilling future.

CAUTIONS

People have occasionally experienced sickness after eating certain varieties. In some cases, this is due to a negative reaction to the mucilaginous quality. There may be other chemical reasons as well. So despite this being a very commonly used food historically for millennia, we suggest you start with a very small amount and monitor your reactions.

PINK FAMILY (CARYOPHYLLACEAE)

The Pink family consists of 83 to 89 genera (depending on which authority) and about 3,000 species worldwide. At least 28 genera are found in Oregon.

CHICKWEED
Stellaria media

The chickweed plant with its small white flowers

A view of the whole chickweed plant

There are 190 species of *Stellaria* worldwide, with at least 11 found in Oregon.

Use: The leaves are best raw in salads but can also be cooked in various dishes or dried and powdered to make into pasta.

Range: Moist and shady areas in urban settings, mountain canyons, and along rivers. Scattered widely where the conditions are ideal.

Similarity to toxic species: You may find young common spurge (*Euphorbia peplus*) in chickweed patches, which superficially resembles chickweed. But spurge doesn't have the line of white hairs, its stalk is more erect, and the leaves are alternate, not opposite like chickweed. If you break the stem of spurge, you will see a white sap; it shouldn't be eaten.

Best time: Spring; chickweed rarely lasts beyond midsummer.

Status: Common

Tools needed: None

A closer view of the chickweed leaves

PROPERTIES

Chickweed is one of the introduced *Stellarias* that is now widespread in Oregon. In fact, today it can be found worldwide. It is common in urban yards, shady fields, and canyons. It is a short-lived annual that shrivels up by summer when the soil is dry.

RECIPE

Mia's Chickweed Soup

Although chickweed can be found in city sidewalks, it's best to gather it in the wild, away from pesticides. As an homage to their humble origins, I call this my "Sidewalk Soup." It's simple, low fat (you can omit the pancetta or bacon and it's still amazing), and has a surprising depth of flavor reminiscent of spring peas and pea shoots. This is my version of "wild split-pea soup."

4–5 tablespoons diced pancetta (or bacon)

1 medium onion, diced

1 stalk celery, diced

1 carrot, diced

1 teaspoon olive oil, as needed

4–5 cloves garlic, finely minced

1 teaspoon fennel seeds

1 small Oregon myrtle leaf

1 small leaf white sage

2 teaspoons French or Italian herbs (I like oregano, thyme, and parsley)

1 small potato, cubed

6 cups packed chickweed, washed and chopped

1 teaspoon raw apple cider vinegar (to keep mixture green)

Salt and pepper to taste

In a heated stockpot, sauté the pancetta or bacon until crisp. Add onion, celery, and carrots and sauté until translucent. You may need to add a bit of olive oil to the bottom of the pan, approximately 1 teaspoon. Add the garlic and spices and continue to sauté until just fragrant. Add the cubed potato; it will serve to thicken the soup, once pureed. Add the chickweed (save a handful for garnish) and enough water to cover the chickweed with an inch of water. Cover and bring to a boil. Add the vinegar, then reduce to a light simmer for about 20–30 minutes.

Once slightly cooled, transfer to a food processor and puree the mixture. Add salt and pepper to taste. Serve with tender, crisp chickweed as garnish. Delish!

—RECIPE FROM MIA WASILEVICH

Nyerges teaches the field students how to recognize chickweed. PHOTO BY RICK ADAMS

Chickweed is a low-growing, sprawling annual that first arises after the winter rains. The thin stem will grow up to a foot long, and upon close inspection you'll see a line of fine white hairs along one side of the stem. The oval-shaped leaves, arranged in pairs along the stem, come to a sharp tip. The flowers are white and 5-petaled, though it may appear to have 10 petals because each flower has a deep cleft.

USES

Chickweed is probably best used as a salad ingredient. In a thick patch of chickweed, one can cut off a handful of the stems just above the root. Then you just rinse the leaves, dice, and add salad dressing.

The plant can also be cooked in soups and stews. For those who are more adventurous, the entire chickweed plant (aboveground) can be dried, powdered, and mixed 50-50 with wheat flour, then run through a pasta machine. The result is a green pasta with a flavor of chickweed.

Because chickweed grows close to the ground with its fine stems, it is common to find other plants growing in chickweed patches. So you need to make certain you are only collecting chickweed. We've seen poison hemlock growing within chickweed patches.

GOOSEFOOT FAMILY (CHENOPODIACEAE)

The Goosefoot family consists of 100 genera and about 1,500 species worldwide, found especially in the deserts and saline or alkaline soils. Some are cultivated for food. There are 13 genera in Oregon.

According to Dr. Leonid Enari, this is one of those very promising plant families for food. His research indicated that most of the leaves could be used for food, either raw or cooked if too bitter and unpalatable. Dr. Enari also stated that the majority of the seeds could be harvested, winnowed, and ground and used for a flour or flour extender.

ORACH
Atriplex hastata

The orach plant. Note its resemblance to lamb's quarters. PHOTO BY RICK ADAMS

There are about 250 species of *Atriplex* worldwide, and about a dozen are found in Oregon, generally known as orach or saltbush. Most are native.

Use: Leaves can be eaten raw if palatable or cooked; dried for a seasoning.
Range: Restricted to the Oregon beaches; can be cultivated
Similarity to toxic species: In the very young stages, one might confuse the nightshade plant, *Solanum nigrum*, with orach.
Best time: Spring
Status: Somewhat common
Tools needed: None

Note the unique triangular configuration of the orach leaves. PHOTO BY RICK ADAMS

A view of the leaf and stem PHOTO BY RICK ADAMS

PROPERTIES

When most folks see orach for the first time, they think it is a lamb's quarter plant with pointy leaves. Orach really does resemble lamb's quarter, except that it is pretty restricted to the coastal regions. Look closely at each leaf. The color is very much like lamb's quarter, except that the leaf has 2 bottom barbs that make

A closer look at the orach leaf PHOTO BY RICK ADAMS

it look very much like an arrowhead. Also, look closely at the young leaves and you will note that the very edge of the leaf has the red tint that you often see in the stems of lamb's quarter.

Orach is found along beaches and in back bays. It grows about 2 feet tall and has inconspicuous flowers.

USES

Orach is used more or less as you'd use lamb's quarter, except it's usually a bit saltier and sometimes more bitter. This means that sometimes you wouldn't use orach in salads, unless very sparingly for that salty flavor. On the other hand, I have eaten raw orach leaves that were mild and tasty and wonderful in salads. The soil, time of year, and age of the plant all seem to play a role in the palatability of orach.

The young orach leaves can be boiled like spinach and eaten alone, and they're very much like cooked lamb's quarter. However, depending on their age when picked, you might find them a bit strong flavored. Changing the water and cooking again usually improves the flavor. The leaves are probably better when added to a mixed green and vegetable stew or soup, or added sparingly to rice or egg dishes.

Try drying and powdering the orach leaves, and then using it as a salt substitute. Use it sparingly at first because it could be very strong.

SEEDS

Though I've not done much with the seeds, other botanical experimenters have harvested and winnowed *Atriplex* seeds and ground them into flour for pastries with good results.

LAMB'S QUARTER, WHITE AND GREEN
Chenopodium album and *C. murale*

Young *Chenopodium album*, or white lamb's quarter

There are about 100 species of *Chenopodium* worldwide, and about 21 species are found in Oregon.

Use: Leaves eaten raw or cooked; seeds added to soups or bread batter; leaves dried for seasoning
Range: Prefers disturbed soils of farms, gardens, hillsides, fields, along trails, etc.
Similarity to toxic species: Black nightshade leaves can be confused with lamb's quarter leaves when very young. Be sure to look for the white mealy (and "sparkly") underside of lamb's quarter, and for the streak of red in the axils.
Best time: Spring for the leaves; late summer for the seeds
Status: Common and widespread
Tools needed: None

PROPERTIES
Lamb's quarter is a plant that everyone has seen but probably not recognized. It's an annual plant that sprouts up in the spring and summer in fields, gardens, and

Young *Chenopodium album*

Young lamb's quarter in the garden

disturbed soils and generally grows about 3 to 4 feet tall. (I did record one at 12 feet, but that's the exception.)

The leaf shape is roughly triangular, somewhat resembling a goose's or duck's foot, hence the family name. The color of the stem and leaves are light green, and the axils of the leaves, and sometimes the stem, are streaked with red. The bottom of each leaf is covered with a mealy substance, causing raindrops to bead up on the leaf.

As the plant matures in the season, the inconspicuous green flowers will appear, and seeds will form as the plant dries and withers.

USES

Lamb's quarter is a versatile plant that can be used in many recipes. The young tender leaves can be cut into smaller pieces and used in a salad. The leaves and tender stems can be cooked like spinach and seasoned for a tasty dish. The water from this cooking makes a delicious broth. The leaves are

The green lamb's quarter (*Chenopodium murale*) with glossy-green leaves

Harvested seed from the *Chenopodium album*

a versatile green, which I've used as an addition to soups, egg dishes, and quiche, and even stir-fried with other vegetables.

Lamb's quarter will go to seed by late summer, and seeds from the dead plant are harvestable for several months. The seed is an excellent source of calcium, phosphorus, and potassium, according to the USDA. Collect the seeds by hand and place in a large salad bowl, then rub them between your hands to remove the chaff. Next, winnow them by letting handfuls drop into the salad bowl as you gently blow off the chaff. The seeds can then be added to soups, rice dishes, and bread batter.

CAUTIONS
Older leaves may cause slight irritation to the throat when eaten raw, without dressing.

Forager note: Everyone should get to know lamb's quarter. Not only is it widespread in Oregon, but it can also be found throughout the world. I once spent a week in the mountains eating only lamb's quarter (salad, soup, fried, boiled). It is a plant that I can depend on finding even during a drought when nothing else is available.

GLASSWORT (a.k.a. PICKLEWEED)
Salicornia spp.

A young glasswort plant growing on the beach PHOTO BY RICK ADAMS

There are about 50 species of *Salicornia* worldwide, but only *S. rubra* is believed to grow in Oregon.

Use: The tender stems can be eaten raw, cooked, or pickled.
Range: Found along the Pacific coast above high tide, along the rivers that feed into the ocean, and in the back-bay areas
Similarity to toxic species: None
Best time: Spring
Status: Common locally
Tools needed: Clippers

PROPERTIES
Glasswort is often found in the back bays and sand flats above the high-tide areas of the Pacific Ocean. I have seen acres of nearly just glasswort in such places. But it will also grow somewhat solitary, and in some of the fields and wild areas not too far from the beaches.

Note the succulent stalks of the glasswort plant. PHOTO BY RICK ADAMS

The plant stems—about ¼ inch thick—have the appearance of swollen fingers, sort of, but not so thick, with distinct joints. The stalks have a pale-green color—almost translucent—and then turn red in the fall. The entire plant rises no more than a foot or so high. There are no apparent leaves. There are flowers and seeds, but these are usually very inconspicuous.

The maturing stalks of glasswort producing seed and turning red PHOTO BY RICK ADAMS

The overall appearance of the plant is of small swollen green stalks, which turn pale red as they mature.

USES

Glasswort makes a good nibble while you're hiking along the beach. It's also good added to salads, but not too much. Just gently pinch the tender tips and add it sparingly to salads, because in volume it may be a bit too strong and overpowering. Be sure to gather it young enough before it gets woody and largely inedible.

Cooked, glasswort's flavor is just right when added to soups, stews, chowders, and even omelettes. I suggest you taste a little first and experiment before adding too much to your dishes. In some cases, you might find that the flavor is greatly improved by boiling the tender stems, pouring off the water, and then adding the glasswort to your various cooked dishes.

I have also enjoyed pickled glasswort. Just collect the tender young sections of the stems, before they get woody on the inside. Pack them loosely in a jar and cover with raw apple cider vinegar, and put the jar in your refrigerator. In about a month they will make a great garnish and side for various dishes. You can also make your glasswort pickles a bit milder by boiling them briefly, rinsing them, and then putting them into a glass jar with vinegar. Another pickling method is to use a salt solution instead of vinegar. Blanche the glasswort, and add about a tablespoon of salt per pint of water. (Yes, there are a lot of details to making good pickles, so if this interests you, be sure to study a good book that's devoted entirely to making pickles. Or better yet, enroll in a class where you learn how to make pickles hands-on.)

HEATH FAMILY (ERICACEAE)

The Heath family contains about 100 genera and 3,000 species worldwide. In Oregon there are 26 genera of this family.

MADRONE
Arbutus menziesii

The madrone leaves PHOTO BY RICK ADAMS

There are about 20 species of *Arbutus*, and the madrone is the only native species found in Oregon.

Use: Edible fruits
Range: Typically found in conifer and oak forests, usually in the lower elevations; most common near the coast
Similarity to toxic species: None
Best time: Summer
Status: Somewhat common
Tools needed: Container to collect fruit

PROPERTIES

Madrone is a shrub or tree, with reddish bark that is typically shedding and curling. The leaves are alternate, leathery, and evergreen. Each leaf is oblong to ovate, from 4 to 5 inches long, with small and shallow serrations. The white or pinkish petals are fused into a very characteristic down-hanging urn shape. The distinctive fruit is round, about an inch diameter, and orange-red. The fruit is papillate, which means it is uniformly covered with small roundish bumps.

A view of the madrone tree PHOTO BY RICK ADAMS   The bark of the madrone tree PHOTO BY RICK ADAMS

This is a somewhat common wild bush or tree along the Oregon coast and in the interior. If you've ever seen the strawberry tree (*Arbutus unedo*), sometimes used as a horticultural plant, you will notice the resemblance between it and the madrone.

The leaves of the strawberry tree and the madrone are somewhat similar. The strawberry tree leaves have more conspicuous teeth, whereas the madrone leaves are a bit larger—around 4 inches in length—and the leaf margin is entire or minutely serrate. The upper surface of the madrone leaf is bright green, and its bottom side is whitish. Madrone has drooping bell- or lantern-shaped flowers, which consist of 5 sepals, 5 petals, 10 stamens, and 1 pistil. Of course, the most conspicuous part of the madrone are the round fruits, about ¼ inch in diameter. They are round, maroon-colored, and covered with bumps. When you cut the fruits in half, you'll see 5 chambers. The texture is much more substantial than a strawberry. The fruit is on the dry side, mealy, and substantial. However, the sugar content is low.

Though it can make a decent nibble, it is definitely improved by soaking in water, and perhaps even cooking it and adding a bit of honey to make a cider. My mentor Dr. Enari used to let his students try the related strawberry tree fruits. He'd say, "Yes, edible, but no flavor."

USES

The manners in which Northern California native peoples used madrone fruits are perhaps still the best ways to enjoy them. The Pomo and Bear River Band ate these berries fresh, as well as roasted, parched, and stored for later use.

An individual madrone leaf PHOTO BY RICK ADAMS

RECIPE

Madrone Tea

A good way to enjoy madrone is to make a beverage from the peels of bark. Margit Roos-Collins, author of *The Flavors of Home*, describes taking about five peelings of the colorful madrone bark (about 3 by 4 inches of bark), putting it into a cup, and pouring boiling water over it. She describes the flavor as mild, like Chinese green tea with a hint of wood. The tea has a cinnamon color. She suggests trying it in different ways: plain, with honey, with milk, with a cinnamon stick, or mixed with other teas.

A cluster of madrone fruits PHOTO BY DAN BAIRD

Immature madrone fruits PHOTO BY DAN BAIRD   Madrone fruits PHOTO BY HUBBARD

The Miwok used madrone like manzanita and made the fruits into a cider. This is done simply by soaking the berries in warm water for a while, straining out the fruit, and then sweetening the water with honey or some other sweetener. The flavor will vary from mildly sweet to almost flavorless, depending on the quality of the fruit you collected, and perhaps how late in the season you collected it.

The Karok dried the fruits then reconstituted them later, and sometimes mixed them with processed manzanita fruit. The Yurok roasted the berries over a fire before eating them, which would be a great way to process them during a camping trip.

From the Ishi Notebook

The anthropologist Theodora Kroeber wrote the classic book *Ishi in Two Worlds* about Ishi, the last of the Yahi people who survived in the wilds of Northern California through the Gold Rush, and finally came into a town in 1911. His story is fascinating. Before he died in 1916, he taught the anthropologists his traditional way of making fire, catching fish, making shelters, making bows and arrows, and hunting. According to Kroeber, "He [Ishi] might imitate the whimpers of a faun by sucking on a madrone leaf folded between his lips. That was sure to bring out one or several does, uneasy for the safety of their young."

MANZANITA
Arctostaphylos spp.

A view of the manzanita fruits and leaves

There are 62 species of *Arctostaphylos* worldwide, with at least 11 found in Oregon.

Use: Berries for beverage and food additive; leaves for medicine
Range: Different species found in the mountains, chaparral, and even the desert
Similarity to toxic species: None
Best time: Approximately September for berries
Status: Relatively widespread
Tools needed: None

PROPERTIES
In Oregon there are at least 11 species of *Arctostaphylos* that we refer to as some sort of "manzanita" or "bearberry." All are native. They typically have characteristic dark-red or maroon-colored bark, often with a shredded look. They appear either as small trees or bushes, or as low-growing ground-cover plants, often vining (such as *A. uva-ursi*).

The leaves are alternate, evergreen, generally round-ovate shaped, and a bit leathery and stiff. The flowers are like little white lanterns or urns that hang from the plant, and the flower parts are usually in 5s. The flowers mature into the round reddish fruits. Fruits vary slightly in color—an orange-yellow to a darker maroon color. Some have a very sticky surface, and some are very dry on the surface.

Manzanita can be found in a wide array of environments, such as rocky slopes, throughout parts of the desert, in woodlands, etc.

A view of the manzanita leaves

USES

Though the manzanita berries are only available seasonally, generally peaking around September, they are sometimes found in abundance and can also be dried for later use. There are some species whose berries are sticky on the surface, and others that are not. I prefer those that are not sticky because lots of dirt doesn't stick to them and less cleaning is needed.

There are several ways to enjoy manzanita berries. The ripened berries

A closer view of manzanita fruits

can simply be brewed in warm water to make a pleasant lemonade-ish drink. There's a sugar content, and it's sour too, and you can enjoy this drink hot or cold—while sitting around the campfire or with a few fruits in your canteen for a trail drink.

Traditionally, the mature and dried berries would be gently ground on a rock, or something like a *molcajete*. The flour, strained from the seeds, can then be used in many ways: added to other bread products (like acorn flour) as an emulsifier or smoothener, added to various batters, or just added to water for a drink.

The seeds can be boiled for a strong vinegar-flavored liquid. You can use this as a substitute vinegar for your salad dressings, or diluted with water and sweetened for a good wild "lemonade."

A view of the sprawling kinnikinnick PHOTO BY ALGIE AU

Kinnikinnick was an old-time smoking mix made from one of the ground-cover manzanitas. I've used many of the leaves this way, just drying and then finely crumbling them. They smoke well and have a decent aroma, and there's no harmful side effect as with tobacco.

Another old-time Native use is to make an infusion from the leaves and drink it to cure

The sprawling kinnikinnick (*Arctostaphylos uva-ursi*) with fruit PHOTO BY BARRY BRECKLING

poison-oak rash. Though I have never had to try this, I have heard some first-hand reports that it worked quickly and effectively.

LEWIS AND CLARK

Of manzanita, Meriwether Lewis wrote, "An evergreen plant which grows on the open plains usually; the natives smoke its leaves, mixed with tobacco; called by the French *Engages* [boatmen] Sacacommis." *Sacacommis* refers to the fruits of *A. uva-ursi*.

William Clark wrote on October 29, 1805, when they were near The Dalles, Oregon, "This chief gave us to eate Sackacommis burries Hasel nuts fish Pounded, and a kind of Bread made of roots."

SALAL
Gaultheria shallon

A view of the overall plant PHOTO BY JOHN DOYEN

The *Gaultheria* genus includes about 130 species, with 3 found in Oregon.

Use: Fruits are eaten.
Range: Salal is found in mixed evergreen forests, redwood forests, and northern coastal scrub. You typically won't find it in wetlands. Found generally along the coast, up to the western edge of the Cascades.
Similarity to toxic species: None
Best time: Summer
Status: Relatively common
Tools needed: Basket for collecting

PROPERTIES

Salal is a native shrub, with ovate leaves that are finely veined. The hanging-lantern-type flowers make the relationship of the salal plant to the manzanita very clear. The flowers appear in a line along the stalk, and then as the berries develop, they are likewise in a line along the stalk. The berries are dark purple

The salal plant in flower PHOTO BY MATT BELOW

Fruit of the salal PHOTO BY LILY JANE TSONG

to more or less blue-black in color. When mature, the end of the fruit has what appears to be a 5-point indented star.

The plant is a low-growing to medium-size evergreen shrub with either spreading or erect stalks. It grows in moist areas, along the margins of forests, in some cases being the most dominant plant. The leaves are alternate, ovate to elliptical, about 3 to 4 inches in length. The leaves are finely toothed, leathery, and conspicuously veined.

Ripe salal fruit PHOTO BY ZOYA AKULOVA

USES

The Pomo, Karok, and other indigenous people are known to have eaten salal berries fresh. These were widely used and were prepared in many different ways. The berries were dried and formed into cakes, which were then saved for later. The cakes would sometimes be dipped into oil and cooked. Or the cakes would be reconstituted by boiling and then eaten. The fruits might also be mixed with other dried berries and stored for winter use. Jam, jellies, and pies were all made from salal.

The Karok also used the fresh fruits as a dye for basket caps, and among other tribes, a switch off the branches was used for making soap from the soapberries.

LEWIS AND CLARK

On December 9 and December 27, 1805, William Clark wrote about the meals that his Native hosts prepared for him where salal was a major ingredient.

HUCKLEBERRY AND BLUEBERRY
Vaccinium spp.

The *Vaccinium* genus includes more than 400 species worldwide, with at least 12 found in Oregon. In general, *Vacciniums* are often referred to as huckleberries, blueberries, cranberries, and even bilberries, depending on the species. Nearly all are native, except *V. macrocarpon*, which is the common cranberry.

Use: The fruits are edible.
Range: *Vacciniums* are forest inhabitants, mostly found in the northern half of the state and farther into the Northwest. They are found in woodland clearings and in the woods themselves, mostly coniferous woods. They like moist and shaded areas and north-facing hills.
Similarity to toxic species: None
Best time: Early spring for flowers; early summer for fruit
Status: Common
Tools needed: Collecting basket

PROPERTIES
These are shrubs, with alternate evergreen to deciduous leaves, which are broadly lance shaped. The stems are trailing to erect. The flower's petals generally number 4 to 5, with a corolla that is cup or urn shaped. The fruit could be red or blue, larger or smaller, and have flattened ends. Generally, the plants with the most desirable fruits are the smaller shrubs, about 3 feet tall, with the larger sweet, juicy blue berries measuring about ¼ to ½ inch diameter.

The fruits of all *Vacciniums* can be eaten, and some are better than others. The best way to make sure you have identified the plant is to observe it when the plant is fruiting, and then take note of the leaf and stem characteristics.

Many species grow in the Northwest, and they are loosely categorized into three groups: those that are found in the bogs and swamps; those that produce the tiny (usually) red berries, which are very sweet but require a lot of time to collect in any appreciable amount, for example, *V. scoparium* (whortleberry); and those that grow in the higher elevations where there is well-drained soil, with dark blue berries, such as *V. globulare*.

HUCKLEBERRY, EVERGREEN
Vaccinium ovatum

This is an evergreen shrub with hairy leaves, 2 to 5 centimeters long, elliptical to lanceolate, and leathery. The 5 sepals are fused at the base. The fruit is about 6 to 9 millimeters long. These grow in the clearings of conifer forests, mostly in

Huckleberry (*Vaccinium ovatum*) in fruit PHOTO BY ZOYA AKULOVA

the western Cascades. According to some early historians, the Karok waited until fall, preferably after a frost, to eat these purple-to-black fruits because they were sweeter then.

LEWIS AND CLARK

On January 27, 1806, Meriwether Lewis wrote, "The natives either eat these berrys when ripe immediately from the bushes or dried in the sun or by means of their sweating kilns; very frequently they pound them and bake them in large loaves of 10 or fifteen pounds; this bread keeps very well during one season and retains the moist jeucies of the fruit much better than by any other method of preservation. This bread is broken and stired in could water until it be sufficiently thick and then eaten; in this way the natives most generally use it."

Blueberry (*V. uliginosum*) PHOTO BY JEAN PAWEK

An overall look at the blueberry plant (*V. uliginosum*) PHOTO BY JEAN PAWEK

Garden blueberry (*V. corymbosum*)

Garden blueberry

HUCKLEBERRY, RED
Vaccinium parvifolium

This one is deciduous, rarely evergreen, with leaves 10 to 25 millimeters, elliptic to ovate, and thin. They are most likely to be found in moist and shaded woodlands of the western Cascades.

These bright-red fruits were eaten fresh by the Karok, Pomo, and Bear River Band in midsummer when they ripened.

BLUEBERRY
Vaccinium uliginosum

The fruits of all species can be eaten raw or cooked. The flavor of the ripe fruit can vary from tart to very sweet. They can be used to makes pies and jellies, cobblers, and preserves. The fruits can also be dried for later use and used to make a fruit pemmican.

The dried leaves can be infused to make a tasty and nutritious tea.

OAK FAMILY (FAGACEAE)

The Oak family includes 7 genera and about 900 species worldwide. There are 3 genera in Oregon.

OAK TREE
Quercus spp.

The Oregon oak (*Q. garryana*) showing the acorn
PHOTO BY JULIE KIERSTEAD NELSON

There are about 600 species of *Quercus* worldwide, with 9 species in Oregon, including *Q. garryana* (Oregon oak), *Q. kelloggii* (black oak), and *Q. chrysolepis* (canyon live oak).

Use: Acorns used for food once leached; miscellaneous craft and dye uses
Range: Oregon oak is mostly in the western Cascades; black oak is found in the foothills and lower mountains.
Similarity to toxic species: The tannic acid in acorns is considered "toxic," but it's so bitter that you'd never eat enough to get sick or cause a problem.
Best time: Acorns mature from mid-September to as late as early February.
Status: Common
Tools needed: Collecting bag

A bowl of the canyon live oak acorns, *Q. chrysolepis*

PROPERTIES
Some oak trees are deciduous and some are evergreen, and the leaf shapes vary from simple to pinnately lobed.

The fruit of all oak trees is the acorn, which every child can recognize. Some acorns are fat, some long and thin, and the caps can vary significantly. Still, the nut set in a scaly cap is universally recognized as the acorn. You should have no trouble recognizing acorns wherever you live.

USES
The acorn is a wonderful source of starchy food. Though I have 3 separate cookbooks devoted entirely to using acorns in the modern kitchen, I generally only use acorns for cookies, pancakes, and bread.

In the old days acorns were an important source of food for Native Americans. Acorns were typically collected and dried, and then stored until needed. The acorns were then shelled, as they are much easier to shell when dried. The acorns would first be ground up, and then placed on a sloping rock with a lip at the lower end, or some other variation of a colander. Cold or hot water poured over the acorn meal would wash out the tannic acid. You'd know it was done by tasting. Then, the meal was mostly used as a thickener in soups and stews, making a type of gravy. Acorns were such an important food that every tribe had their own way of processing them, so there was a lot of variety in how this would have been done.

Grinding acorns on a flat metate, right, and the stone bowl molcajete, left

After the acorn flour is put into a cloth, which is sitting in a colander, water is poured through the flour until the flour is no longer bitter.

There was much lore surrounding the various types of acorns; the acorn meal sometimes had a religious significance and would have been used in various ceremonies, in much the way that corn or corn pollen is used.

The availability of acorns to tribes was as important in their social development as was agriculture to other cultures. Acorns were a more or less guaranteed food source, and thus provided a stable foundation upon which the other aspects of the society could flower. And you didn't just go collect acorns wherever you wanted: Families controlled the various oak groves, and thus controlled access to the acorns, which represented political power.

Today, on the trail or in the kitchen, the neatest and quickest way to process acorns is to boil them, changing the water repeatedly until they are no longer bitter. Then, while still wet, I prefer to process them through a hand-crank meat grinder to produce a coarse meal. Ground finer, which you can do in a coffee grinder once the meal is dry, the meal is perfect for any product calling for flour. I typically mix the acorn flour 50-50 with wheat or other flour. This is partly for flavor and partly because acorn flour doesn't hold together as well as, for example, wheat flour.

The more traditional method of processing first involves shelling the acorns, and then grinding them while still raw. I typically do this on a large flat-rock metate. Then the meal is put into some sort of primitive colander and water (hot or cold) is poured through it. There were many possible ways to create a colander in the old days; today I just put a cotton cloth inside a large colander and pour cold water over it. The water takes awhile to trickle out, and it may require several pourings of water before the acorn meal is no longer bitter and can be eaten.

I have had modern acorn products of chips, pound cake, and pasta, and they are delicious. If I had to describe the acorn flavor, I would say that products made with acorn have a subtle graham cracker flavor.

How good are acorns for you? Here are some details from a chart that was published in *Temalpakh: Cahuilla Indian Knowledge and Usage of Plants* by Lowell John Bean and Katherine S. Saubel. Their source was Martin A. Baumhoff, *Ecological Determinants of Aboriginal California Populations* (Berkeley: University of California Press, 1936, p. 162), as modified by

Buddy and Gary Gonzales cooking acorn pancakes

Carl Brandt Wolf, *California Wild Tree Crops* (Claremont, CA: Rancho Santa Ana Botanic Garden, 1945, table 1), and W. S. Spector, *Handbook of Biological Data* (Philadelphia and London: W. B. Saunders Co., 1956, table 156).

CHEMICAL COMPOSITION OF HULLED ACORNS (in percent)

Species	Water	Protein	Fats	Fiber	Carbohydrates	Ash	Total Proteins, Fats, Carbohydrates
Q. lobata	9.0	4.9	5.5	9.5	69.0	2.1	79
Q. garryana	9.0	3.9	4.5	12.0	68.9	1.8	77
Q. douglasii	9.0	5.5	8.1	9.8	65.5	2.1	79
Q. chrysolepis	9.0	4.1	8.7	12.7	63.5	2.0	76
Q. agrifolia	9.0	6.3	16.8	11.6	54.6	1.8	78
Q. kelloggii	9.0	4.6	18.0	11.4	55.5	1.6	78
Barley	10.1	8.7	1.9	5.7	71.0	2.6	82
Wheat	12.5	12.3	1.8	2.3	69.4	1.7	84

RECIPE

Northwest Memories

Use processed acorn flour (with tannic acid removed), mixed half-and-half with wheat flour, and an appropriate amount of water. The dough is then formed into small loaves and cooked on a soapstone slab.

GERANIUM FAMILY (GERANIACEAE)

Worldwide, there are 6 genera and about 750 species in this family. In Oregon this family is represented by 3 genera.

FILAREE
Erodium spp.

A view of the filaree plant

There are about 74 species of *Erodium* worldwide, and 4 are found in Oregon.

Use: The leaves are eaten raw, cooked, or juiced.

Range: Prefers lawns, fields, cultivated and disturbed soils, and the fringes of the urban wilderness

Similarity to toxic species: Since filaree superficially resembles a fern, and perhaps a member of the Carrot or Parsley family (when not in flower), make sure you are thoroughly familiar with filaree before eating any.

Best time: Spring

Status: Somewhat common

Tools needed: None

PROPERTIES

Filaree is a very common urban weed, found in gardens, grasslands, and fields. This annual plant grows as a low-growing rosette of pinnately compound leaves, which are covered with short hairs. The stalk is fleshy. Sometimes people will think they are looking at a fern when they see filaree. The small 5-petaled flowers of spring are purple, followed by the very characteristic needlelike fruits.

USES

First, I'm well aware that many gardeners and landscapers hate this introduced plant. It is persistent and sometimes widespread. It seems to grow in even the worst soils. Still, it's edible, and when properly prepared, it's good!

Filaree leaves and stalks can be picked when young and enjoyed in

The linear seed capsules of the maturing filaree

The filaree flower PHOTO BY RICK ADAMS

The young rosette of the filaree

salads. The leaves are a little fibrous but sweet. I pick the entire leaf, including the long stem, for salads or other dishes. They are best chopped up before added to salads or cooked dishes such as soups or stews.

You might also enjoy simply picking the tender stems and chewing on them. They are sweet and tasty, somewhat reminiscent of celery. In fact, sometimes in a dry year, I find that the stem is the only part that I will eat. The leafy section is drier and more fibrous and lends itself better to being added to a stew.

In wet seasons the spring growth of filaree is more succulent and tasty. In dry years the season will be short and the leaves and stems of filaree will be less desirable.

RECIPE

Filaree-Up My Cup

If you have a wheatgrass juicer, you can process some filaree leaves and then enjoy the sweet green juice without the fiber.

GOOSEBERRY FAMILY (GROSSULARIACEAE)

This family includes only the *Ribes* genus. There are 120 species worldwide, with more than 2 dozen in Oregon, not including varieties. These are found in all environments.

CURRANTS AND GOOSEBERRIES
Ribes spp.

Ripe and ripening currant fruits. Note the dried flower that typically persists on the end of the fruit.

Use: The fruits are eaten raw, dried, or cooked/processed into juice, jam, and jelly.

Range: Found in the mountains, in flat plains, along rivers, etc.

Similarity to toxic species: When seeing currants for the first time, some folks think they're looking at poison oak—they've heard the saying "Leaflets three, let it be." But the currant has 3 lobes per leaf, not 3 distinct leaflets as does poison oak.

Best time: The fruits are available in mid-spring.

Status: Common locally

Tools needed: None

A view of the fruits and leaves of the currant plant PHOTO BY RICK ADAMS

PROPERTIES

Currants and gooseberries are both the same genus, and so we'll address them together. Both are low shrubs, mostly long vining shoots that arise from the base. The gooseberries have thorns on the stalks and fruits, and the currants do not.

The leaves look like little 3- to 5-fingered mittens. The fruits of both currants and gooseberries hang from the stalks, with the withered flower usually still adhering to the end of the fruit.

You will find currants or gooseberries throughout the diverse ecosystems of Oregon.

USES

Though the straight shoots of currants make excellent arrow shafts, currants and gooseberries are mostly regarded as a great fruit, either eaten raw as a snack, dried, or cooked into various recipes.

A shoot of the currant plant. The straight shoots, once cut, dried, and further straightened, were used in the past for arrow shafts.

Gooseberries are a bit more work to eat since they're covered with tiny spines. I have mashed them and then strained the pulp through a sieve or fine colander. Then I used it as a jelly for pancakes.

Currants require no preparation, so they can be picked off the stalks and eaten fresh. But make sure they are ripe—they'll be a bit tart otherwise.

Army veteran Mark Tsunokai examines a currant with ripening fruit in the field.

Ripe currant fruits

In the old days the currant was a valuable fruit, dried and powdered and added to dried meats as a sugar preservative. Today you can just dry the fruits into simple trail snacks. Or you can collect a lot and make jams or jellies, or even delicious drinks. And though the currant leaf is not usually regarded as an important food source, some can be eaten in salads or cooked dishes for a bit of vitamin C. They are a bit tough as they get older.

Rule of thumb on the *Ribes* fruits: If it tastes good, it's good to eat. None are poisonous, but not all are palatable.

CAUTIONS
Be sure you've identified currant or gooseberry and that you can tell the difference between these and poison oak.

LEWIS AND CLARK
On April 16, 1805, Meriwether Lewis wrote, "Among others there is a currant which is now in blume and has yellow blossom something like the yellow currant of the Missouri but it is a different species." Botanists believe that Lewis was describing *R. aureum*. Lewis also writes, "I find these fruits very pleasant particularly the yellow currant which I think vastly preferable to those of our gardens. . . . The fruit is a berry. . . . It is quite as transparent as the red current of our gardens, not so ascid, & more agreeably flavored."

MINT FAMILY (LAMIACEAE)

The Mint family has about 230 genera and about 7,200 species worldwide. In Oregon we have examples from 28 genera, many of which are food and medicine.

MINT
Mentha spp.

This closeup of the mint plant shows opposite leaves, wrinkly leaves, and a square stem.

There are 18 species of *Mentha* worldwide, with 7 found in Oregon.

Use: As a beverage
Range: Along rivers and wet areas; often cultivated and escaping cultivation
Similarity to toxic species: None
Best time: Mint can be collected at any time.
Status: Not common
Tools needed: None

PROPERTIES

Our wild mints in Oregon include spearmint (*M. spicata*), peppermint (*M. piperita*), and field mint (*M. arvensis*). Of our state's 7 wild mints, 4 are natives. In the wild, mints are typically found along streams. They are sprawling, vining

Wild mints

plants with squarish stems and finely wrinkled opposite leaves. Crush the leaf for the unmistakable clue to identification. If you have a good sense of smell, you'll detect the obvious minty aroma.

Peppermint and spearmint are usually cultivated in gardens. They sometimes escape cultivation and are found in marshes, ditches, meadows, around lakes, and in other moist areas.

The white, pink, or violet flowers of *Mentha* are clustered in tight groups along the stalk, often appearing like balls on the stems. The flowers, though 5-petaled, consist of an upper 2-lobed section and a lower 3-lobed section.

USES

The wild mints are not primarily a food but are excellent sources for an infused tea. Put the fresh leaves into a cup or pot, boil some water, and then pour the water over the leaves. Cover the cup and let it sit awhile. I enjoy the infusion plain, but you might prefer to add honey, lemon, or some other flavor.

We've had some campouts where we had very little food and were relying on fishing and foraged food. Even in off-seasons in the mountains, we were able to find wild mint and make a refreshing tea. The aroma is invigorating and helps to open the sinuses. The flavor and taste of mint tea seems even more enjoyable when camping. Also, you can just crush some fresh leaves and add them to your canteen while hiking. It makes a great cold trail beverage and requires no sweeteners.

Sometimes we add the fresh leaves to trout while it is cooking. They add a great flavor. If used sparingly, you can dice up the fresh leaves and add them to salads for a refreshing minty flavor. Of course, they can be diced and added to various dessert dishes, like ice cream, sherbet, etc. Or you can try adding a few sprigs of mint to your soups and stews to liven up the flavor. And if you really want to try something special for your doomsday parties, add a little fresh mint to your favorite pouch of MRE.

Mints are also great breath-fresheners. Just chew on a few fresh leaves.

Wild mint in the field PHOTO BY JEFF MARTIN

Aromatic mints are also good for a mouthwash. Make an infusion of any fresh mint that you enjoy, about a quarter cup of fresh leaves to each quart of water. When cool, strain, and keep refrigerated until needed.

MEDICINE

If you have a mildly upset stomach, try some mint tea before reaching for some fizzy pill. Mint tea has a well-deserved reputation for calming an upset stomach. The Ojibwa people used the tea to help reduce fevers.

MALLOW FAMILY (MALVACEAE)

The Mallow family includes 266 genera and about 4,025 species worldwide. There are 10 genera represented in Oregon, including hibiscus.

According to Dr. Leonid Enari, the Mallow family is a safe family for wild-food experimentation. He cautions, however, that some species may be too fibrous to eat.

MALLOW
Malva neglecta

Young mallow growing out of a thick bed of chickweed

There are 30 to 40 species of Malva worldwide, with 5 found in Oregon.

Use: Leaves raw, cooked, or dried (for tea); "cheeses" eaten raw or cooked; seeds cooked and eaten like rice
Range: Urban areas such as fields, disturbed soils, and gardens
Similarity to toxic species: None
Best time: Spring
Status: Common and widespread
Tools needed: None

A view of the round mallow leaves and its shallow lobes

Note the round seed clusters of the mallow, also called "cheeses."

PROPERTIES

These plants resemble geraniums with their rounded leaves. Each leaf's margin is finely toothed, and there is a cleft to the middle of the leaf to which the long stem is attached. If you look closely, you'll see a red spot where the stem meets the leaf.

The flowers are small but attractive, composed of 5 petals, generally colored white to blue, though some could be lilac or pink. The flowers are followed by the round flat fruits, which gave rise to the plant's other name, "cheeseweed."

These plants are indeed widespread. In the late winter and spring, they're mostly in urban terrain and on the fringes.

USES

When you take a raw leaf and chew on it, you will find it becomes a bit mucilaginous. For this reason, it is used to soothe a sore throat. In Mexico you can find the dried leaf under the Spanish name *malva* at herb stores, sold as a medicine. Though the entire plant is edible, the stalks and leaf stems tend to be a bit fibrous, so I just use the leaf and discard the stem. These are good added to salads, though they are a bit tough for the only salad ingredient.

The mallow leaf is also good in cooked dishes—soups, stews, or finely chopped for omelettes and stir-fries. I have even seen some attempts to use larger mallow leaves as a substitute for grape leaves in dolmas, which is cooked rice wrapped in a grape leaf. I thought it worked out pretty well.

In this hillside where old tires have been used as a stairway, mallow grows out of the steps every spring.

As this plant flowers and matures, the flat and round seed clusters appear. When still green, these make a good nibble. The green "cheeses" (as they are commonly called) can be added raw to salads, cooked in soups, or even pickled into capers. Once the plant is fully mature and the leaves are drying up, you can collect the now-mature cheeses. The round clusters will break up into individual seeds, which you can winnow and then cook like rice. Though the cooked seeds are a bit bland, they are reminiscent of rice. Because mallow is so very common, it would not be hard to prepare a dish of the mallow seed. To really improve the flavor, try mixing the mallow seeds with quinoa, buckwheat groats, or couscous. The root of the related marsh mallow (*Althaea officinalis*) was once the source for making marshmallows, which are now just another junk food. Originally, the roots were boiled until the water was gelatinous. The water would be whipped to thicken it and then sweetened. You'd then have a spoonful to treat a cough or sore throat. Yes, you can use the common mallow's roots to try this, though it doesn't get quite as thick as the original.

MINER'S LETTUCE FAMILY (MONTIACEAE)

The Miner's Lettuce family includes 22 genera with about 230 species worldwide. There are at least 6 genera represented in Oregon.

Dr. Leonid Enari regarded this as a completely safe family for wild-food experimentation. He taught that all members could be eaten, usually raw, but sometimes needing to be steamed or cooked for improved palatability. Dr. Enari also taught that the seeds of most could be harvested and eaten.

SPRING BEAUTY
Claytonia lanceolata

The spring beauty plant PHOTO BY KEIR MORSE

There are 27 species of *Claytonia* worldwide, with 13 found in Oregon. This genus was formerly referred to as *Montia*.

Use: The entire plant, including the bulbs, can be eaten.
Range: Widespread from Canada, east to the Rockies, south to central California. In Oregon expect to find it mostly in open fields and subalpine meadows, mainly in the Cascades.
Similarity to toxic species: None
Best time: Spring. It's one of the first spring plants that can be eaten.
Status: Relatively common locally
Tools needed: Bag for leaves, trowel for tubers

PROPERTIES

Spring beauty is a perennial herb that grows no more than about 6 inches tall. There is a little root—like a small radish up to an inch in diameter. One or more stalks will grow from each little bulb.

The leaves are all more or less basal, appearing in the spring and summer. The linear to lance-shaped leaves are about 2½ to 4 inches long, and they are arranged opposite each other. Remember, this is related to miner's lettuce, and the color, texture, and feel of the spring beauty leaf is very much like its relative. The small white flowers often have pink veins and are about 5 to 12 millimeters wide.

The flowering spring beauty
PHOTO BY CHRISTIE

Spring beauty is found mostly in subalpine areas, even at the edges of snowmelt. This is a wilderness plant, not one you'll find in urban fields or in your backyard. Once, however, when pulled over to the side of the road at a high-elevation location, I found spring beauty growing in a little patch of moist soil between the road and the abutting mountain.

USES

Spring beauty leaves are pleasant to all palates and can be used as a main salad ingredient or mixed with other greens. They are also great just cooked like spinach. You can try them in egg dishes and soups. The flavor is

Spring beauty, *Claytonia sibirica* PHOTO BY SCHUSTEFF

mild and the texture is spinach-like, so these greens will go well with most dishes.

The little starchy bulbs can be dug, but I generally just leave them alone. In heavily traveled areas, I have seen certain wild foods "dry up" until the area has had a chance to recover. Yes, these bulbs are good—mild, tasty, and nutritious. The bulbs are down about 6 inches at least, and you can carefully dig them out with a little trowel.

But be an ecological forager. Don't deplete a patch, and do your best to keep the area looking natural, and even better than when you found it!

LEWIS AND CLARK

As most Oregonians know, the Lewis and Clark expedition passed along the Columbia River and dipped into Oregon. According to the journal kept by Captain Lewis, in an entry dated June 25, 1806: "I met with a plant the root of which the Shoshones eat. It is a small knob root a good deel in flavor an consistency like the Jerusalem artichoke." He was speaking of the spring beauty tubers.

MINER'S LETTUCE
Claytonia perfoliata

SIBERIAN MINER'S LETTUCE
Claytonia sibirica

Miner's lettuce. The flower stalk arises from the cup-like leaf. PHOTO BY RICK ADAMS

There are 27 species of *Claytonia* worldwide, with 13 found in Oregon. This genus was formerly referred to as *Montia*.

Use: Entire aboveground plant can be eaten raw, boiled, steamed, sautéed, or added to soup, eggs, etc.
Range: Mostly found in moist canyons below 3,000 feet, on both sides of the Cascades, with *C. perfoliata* more common
Similarity to toxic species: None
Best time: Spring
Status: Common seasonally
Tools needed: None

PROPERTIES
Miner's lettuce was one of the very first wild foods that I learned to identify. I'd seen the characteristic leaf—a round cuplike leaf with the flower stalk growing out of the middle—in Bradford Angier's *Free for the Eating*. It was just one drawing, but I was certain I'd be able to recognize it. One day I got a phone call from

Young miner's lettuce sprouts in the field.

A view of a cluster of miner's lettuce

a fellow budding forager, and he told me that he'd spotted the plant in the local mountains. I bicycled to the site that afternoon, climbed up the hillside, and sure enough, I found it!

That night I tried my first miner's lettuce in salad and some boiled like spinach. It was good, but perhaps the experience was a bit anticlimactic because I was so wrapped up in the lore and history of the plant. I didn't realize there'd be nothing really incredible about the plant—just a tasty though somewhat bland leaf that could be used in many ways.

Miner's lettuce leaves are formed in a rosette, with each leaf arising from the root. The young leaves are linear, and the older ones are somewhat triangular to quadrangular in shape, with some appearing water-spotted. The key characteristic is the flowering stalk with its pink or white 5-petaled flowers, which arise from a cup-shaped leaf. Clusters of these unique cup-shaped leaves, all arising from a common root like a head of leaf lettuce, make this a very easy plant to recognize.

USES

It seems that everyone in Oregon knows miner's lettuce. This is probably because the plant is so distinctive—when

Miner's lettuce in the field

it's in flower, you really can't confuse it for anything else. Plus, it tastes good, it often grows very abundantly, and it's easy to work with. Think of the plant as a somewhat succulent lettuce that is also good cooked, and you'll get some idea how versatile this plant can be.

Flavor- and texture-wise, this is perhaps one of my favorite wild foods. My brother Richard always regarded it as his favorite. We have used it in many recipes—just think of all the diverse ways in which we use common spinach!

To give some examples of the many ways in which we can eat miner's lettuce, consider a weekend survival trip I once led for a dozen young men. Our only food was what we fished or foraged, and there was very little growing in the area besides miner's lettuce. We had miner's lettuce salad, miner's lettuce soup, fried miner's lettuce, boiled miner's lettuce, miner's lettuce cooked with fish, and miner's lettuce broth! If we were in a kitchen with all sorts of condiments, we'd have had miner's lettuce omelettes and soufflés and stir-fries and green drinks.

In other words, in any recipe—raw, cooked, or juiced—that calls for "greens," you can use miner's lettuce.

RECIPE

Richard's Salad

This is my brother Richard's recipe. He lived in Portland for part of the year, working as a welder for the Rose Festival, and made miner's lettuce salads whenever possible in the spring.

Rinse 4 cups of miner's lettuce leaves. Mix with a dressing of equal parts cold-pressed olive oil and raw apple cider vinegar, to which you can add a dash of garlic powder and paprika, to taste. Richard sometimes topped his salad with sliced hard-boiled eggs.

EVENING PRIMROSE FAMILY (ONAGRACEAE)

The Evening Primrose family has 22 genera and about 657 species worldwide. There are 16 genera of this family in Oregon.

FIREWEED
Chamerion angustifolium

The maturing fireweed plants producing their seed capsules PHOTO BY RON AND ANTHONY BANIAGA

There are 2 species of *Chamerion* in Oregon. This genus was formerly known as *Epilobium*.

Use: Leaves and tender portions are edible.
Range: Widespread, though more common in western Oregon
Similarity to toxic species: Could be confused with other plants when not in flower, but when fireweed is in flower, it cannot be confused with anything else.
Best time: Spring
Status: Common in certain areas, especially in burned or clear-cut areas. A known fire-follower.
Tools needed: Clippers to collect tender stems

PROPERTIES

As the common name implies, fireweed is a fire-follower, often sprouting up in large patches in areas that have recently burned. The species name *angustifolium*

The leaves of the fireweed plant PHOTO BY RON AND ANTHONY BANIAGA

The flowers of fireweed PHOTO BY RON AND ANTHONY BANIAGA

(narrow-leaved) is constructed from the Latin words *angustus* for "narrow" and *folium* for "leaf."

The reddish stems of this herbaceous perennial are usually erect, smooth, and arise from 2 to nearly 8 feet tall. Alternately arranged leaves are lanceolate and

Flowering fireweed in the field PHOTO BY SIMON TONGE

Closeup of the stunning fireweed flowers PHOTO BY RON AND ANTHONY BANIAGA

more or less pinnately veined. The flowers have 4 magenta-to-pink petals, 2 to 3 centimeters in diameter. The styles have 4 stigmas, and there are 8 stamens.

The reddish-brown linear seed capsule splits from its apex. It bears hundreds of minute brown seeds, which blow about and spread the plant. Fireweed also spreads by its underground roots and eventually forms a large patch.

USES

The very youngest shoots can be snapped off and boiled or steamed like asparagus. The young shoots were collected in the spring by various Native peoples and cooked alone or mixed with other greens.

As the plant matures, the leaves become tough and somewhat bitter, but they could still be cooked to make them more palatable. The stems of the older plant can be peeled and eaten raw. Fireweed is a good source of vitamin C and vitamin A.

A tea made from the mature leaves has been used as a laxative. Blackfoot people crushed the root and made it into a poultice to treat various skin problems like burns, cuts, and abrasions.

Various candies and jellies, and even ice cream, are made today in Alaska from the fireweed plant. OK, so the jelly is not a "health food," but you might be able to tweak the recipe somehow and use a better sugar.

Fireweed Jelly

Gakona Baby of Alaska makes several batches of fireweed jelly each summer when the fireweed is in bloom. Gakona says that it is important that only the blooms be harvested, and not the stems. Also, she has tried this recipe with Certo and it does not set, so be sure to use Sure-Jell or a powdered pectin.

2½ cups fireweed juice (see below)

1 teaspoon lemon juice

½ teaspoon butter

1 (1¾ ounce) package dry pectin

3 cups sugar

Begin by making fireweed juice. Harvest about 8 packed cups of fireweed flowers, rinse thoroughly, and put in a 2-quart pot. Add just enough water so the water level is just below the top of the flowers. When finished, the juice should be a deep-purple color—if it is brownish, too much water was used in the boiling process. Boil the flowers in water until the color is boiled out and the petals are a grayish color. Ladle the juice into a jar through cheesecloth to strain.

Warm the fireweed juice, lemon juice, and butter on the stovetop. Add the pectin, bring to a boil, and boil hard for 1 minute.

Add the sugar and bring to full boil for 1 minute. Skim the top of the jelly. Pour into a pitcher (making it easier to fill the jars) and skim again. Fill sterilized jars, leaving ⅛ inch of space at the top. Process in a hot water bath for 10 minutes.

Yields four 8-ounce jars.

—RECIPE FROM GAKONA BABY

OXALIS FAMILY (OXALIDACEAE)

Though the Oxalis family contains 5 genera and 880 species worldwide, in Oregon it is represented only by the *Oxalis* genus.

SOUR GRASS (a.k.a. WOOD SORREL)
Oxalis spp.

A view of the leaves and flowers of sour grass

There are up to 950 species of *Oxalis* worldwide. At least 8 are found in Oregon.

Use: Everything can be used. Aboveground leaves and stems can be eaten raw, cooked, or pickled. The tiny tubers can also be eaten cooked.

Range: Some are very common in urban settings, while others are found in mountains, meadows, and fields.

Similarity to toxic species: None

Best time: Generally, spring

Status: Common in urban areas

Tools needed: None

PROPERTIES

Sour grass is widespread, and most gardeners hate it because it is such a successful plant. It spreads readily, and if it grows in your yard, there's probably much more than you're likely to use for food.

The tiny tuber of *Oxalis*

The leaves arise from thin stems, and each leaf appears to be 3 hearts connected at the apex of the hearts! Some leaves appear to be water-spotted. The flower stalks are typically taller than the leaves. The flower colors vary from white to pink to yellow. If you dig around under the plant, you'll see some of the tiny tubers of the plant, typically no bigger than a pea.

This is one of the plants commonly referred to as a shamrock, or four-leaf clover. However, oxalis is not a clover and is not related to clover. Typically, each leaf of oxalis is divided into the 3 heart-shaped leaflets, though you will occasionally find 4 leaflets.

USES

Yes, this makes a good trail nibble, but you really can't eat a lot—it's just too sour because of the plant's oxalic acid. But everyone likes this plant. Children rarely refuse sour grass. It's a great snack and livens up other foods.

Use the leaves sparingly in salads for a vinegar flavor. I prefer the flower stalks, but everything aboveground can be used. Everything aboveground can also be cooked into soups or stews, but again, add it sparingly. If it's a bit too strong, boil the plant, rinse the water, and then use.

I've had some fermented sour grass that was made just as you'd make sauerkraut with cabbage. Though it was very stringy, it was still tasty.

Forager note: There is a variety of Oxalis called oca (O. tuberosa) that has long been cultivated in its native Peru, Bolivia, and Ecuador. These tubers measure just a few inches and are very acidic when fresh. They are dried in the sun for a few days to improve the flavor. When they are dried for a few weeks, the flavor is said to resemble figs. So, at the very least, when you see the little tubers under the Oregon species, you can try them as a nibble, or experiment with cooking or drying them.

LOPSEED FAMILY (PHRYMACEAE)

The Lopseed family contains 15 genera worldwide, with 230 species. In Oregon there are 5 genera of this family. *Mimulus* had formerly been classified in the Figwort family.

YELLOW MONKEY FLOWER
Mimulus guttatus

A close-up of the flower PHOTO BY LILY JANE TSONG

There are about 100 species worldwide of *Mimulus*, with 19 in Oregon.

Use: Everything tender above the water line
Range: Found in slow-moving waters or ponds, up to the timberline
Similarity to toxic species: None
Best time: Spring
Status: Common in some areas; not particularly widespread
Tools needed: None

PROPERTIES

This is a common yellow wildflower that grows along the shallow banks of streams, in much the same environment as watercress. It's usually very conspicuous when in flower and fairly easy to recognize.

The bright-yellow flowers are typically on a raceme, with 5 or so flowers per stalk. The flower is composed of an upper lip with 2 lobes and a lower lip with 3 lobes, which also may have many red-to-brown spots or just one large spot. The opening to the tubular flower is hairy. The leaves are opposite, round to oval in shape, usually with irregular teeth.

The monkey flower plant and flowers

The plant may be an annual or perennial, with the stems either erect or sprawling in the water. It's a highly variable plant.

USES

Since the yellow monkey flower grows in slow-moving waters, make sure that the water is clean if you plan to use it in salads.

We've used the leaves and tender stems in salads many times. In general, we just pinch off the tender sections that are above the water. If the water seems impure, be sure to only use these greens in cooked dishes.

The texture is good and the flavor is mild to bland, so it makes a good addition to salads, either alone or mixed with a variety of other wild greens for a balanced flavor. Add some tomatoes and avocado too. Of course, I nearly always add salad dressing to make it tasty, and the salad will have the flavor of whatever salad dressing you use.

The greens also lend themselves well to various cooked dishes. You can simply boil them like spinach, or you can try stir-frying them with other greens and vegetables. You can also make a good rice dish with monkey flower. Cook a pot of brown rice, and when it is nearly done, add some rinsed and diced greens of the monkey flower. Season with butter or a quality soy sauce.

Yellow monkey flower is mild and can always go into any soup or stew pot.

PLANTAIN FAMILY (PLANTAGINACEAE)

The Plantain family has 110 genera and approximately 2,000 species worldwide. There are 18 genera found in Oregon.

PLANTAIN
Plantago major and *P. lanceolata*

Broadleaf plantain

There are about 250 species of *Plantago* worldwide, with about 14 found in Oregon.

Use: Young leaves used for food; seeds used for food and medicine
Range: Prefers lawns, fields, and wet areas
Similarity to toxic species: None
Best time: Spring for the leaves and late summer for the seeds
Status: Fairly common
Tools needed: None

PROPERTIES

Plantain is as common an urban weed as dandelion, though not as widely known. It's usually found in lawns and fields, but also in wet areas.

All the leaves radiate from the base in a rosette fashion, with the basal leaves typically from about 2 to to 6 inches in length. *P. lanceolata*'s leaves are narrow, prominently ribbed with parallel veins. *P. major* has broad glabrous leaves, up to 6 inches long, roundish or ovate shaped. Both have leaves that are covered with soft short hairs.

A patch of broadleaf plantain in a lawn

The flowers are formed in spikes (somewhat resembling a miniature cattail flower spike), usually just a few inches long, and on stems that are typically no more than a foot tall. Each greenish flower is composed of 4 sepals, a small corolla, and 4 stamens (sometimes 2). The flowers are covered by dry, scarious bracts. When the spikes are dry, you can strip off the seeds and winnow them.

USES
The young tender leaves of spring are the best to eat; use in salads or as you would spinach. The leaves that have become more fibrous with age need longer cooking, and they are best finely chopped or pureed and cooked in a cream sauce. The leaves have a mild laxative effect.

The seeds can be eaten once cleaned by winnowing. Harvest the seeds when the stalks are brown and mature. I typically rub them between my hands to remove the outer coatings. I put the seeds into a shallow salad bowl and gently blow onto the seeds so that the chaff blows away.

The seeds can be ground into flour and used as you would regular flour, or soaked in water (to soften) and then cooked like rice. Once cooked, the seeds are slightly mucilaginous and bland.

They can be eaten plain or flavored with honey, butter, or other seasoning.

Cooked plantain leaves have been used as a direct poultice on boils. Plantain is a vulnerary (promotes healing) and is noted for its styptic, antiseptic, and astringent qualities. Native people used the cooked leaves as a poultice for wounds.

Narrowleaf plantain

Narrowleaf plantain with human scale

Plantain leaf, crushed or chopped and used as a poultice, is perhaps the best herb to use for puncture wounds to the body (knife wound, stepping on a nail, etc.). Early American colonists used plantain on insect and venomous reptile bites and used the seeds for expelling worms.

Seeds of the narrowleaf plantain (*P. lanceolata*)

VERONICA (a.k.a. SPEEDWELL)
Veronica americana

A view of the veronica plant growing in water

The *Veronica* genus has about 250 species worldwide, 18 of which are found in Oregon.

Use: The entire plant (tender stems and leaves) above the root can be eaten.
Range: Grows in slow-moving waters, in the same environment as watercress
Similarity to toxic species: None
Best time: Spring and summer
Status: Somewhat common
Tools needed: None

PROPERTIES
Veronica americana is a native and is frequently confused with watercress because they both grow in water. But the resemblance of watercress to veronica is only superficial because there are some obvious differences.

The veronica has a simple leaf about 1 or 2 inches long, whereas the watercress has pinnately divided leaves very much like many of the members of the mustard family. The watercress has a typical mustard flower formula with the 4

View of the veronica plant

The asymmetrical veronica flower
PHOTO BY RICK ADAMS

petals arranged like a cross, and its color is white. But the veronica flower is lavender and asymmetrical with 4 petals, the upper one being wider than the others.

USES

If I have no concerns about the water's safety from which I've picked the veronica, I add it to salads. It is not strongly flavored, and you can use the entire plant. Just pinch it off at water level (no need to uproot the plant), rinse it, and then dice it into your salad. No need to pick off just the leaves—eat the entire above-water plant (both stems and leaves). Since it is bland, you can mix it with stronger-flavored greens in your salad. It goes well with watercress, as well as any of the mustards.

Veronica also goes well with soup dishes and stir-fries. It never gets strongly bitter, like watercress, and it never really gets fibrous. It's a mild plant that's fairly widespread in waterways.

If you live near a waterway where veronica grows, you'll find that it's a good plant to use in a variety of dishes where you might otherwise include spinach. Try some gently sautéed with green onions and add some eggs to make an omelette. Try a cream soup into which you've gently cooked some veronica greens.

BUCKWHEAT FAMILY (POLYGONACEAE)

The Buckwheat family has 48 genera and about 1,200 species worldwide. Eleven of these genera are found in Oregon.

AMERICAN BISTORT
Bistorta bistortoides

The American bistort plant, showing the leaves and flower stalk PHOTO BY DEBRA COOK

The flower stalk of the American bistort PHOTO BY DEBRA COOK

The genus *Bistorta* includes about a dozen species in Oregon. This plant was formerly referred to as *Polygonum bistortoides*.

Use: Edible leaf, root, and seed
Range: Moist meadows and forest clearings, from the foothills to above timberline
Similarity to toxic species: When not in flower, could easily be confused for another, possibly toxic, plant
Best time: Leaves and roots in spring; seeds in late summer
Status: Common
Tools needed: Trowel

PROPERTIES
These are perennial herbs with stems rising from 2 to 8 feet tall. Leaves have long stalks, with the blade up to 6 inches long. Most of the leaves are basal, and the leaves that appear on the flower stalks are shorter and thinner. The leaves are elliptic to lanceolate-oblong. The rhizomes are contorted.

The flowering American bistort in the field
PHOTO BY BOB SWEATT

USES
All members of *Bistorta* are edible, though palatability varies. The root of *B. bistortoides* can be eaten raw or cooked (boiled, baked, roasted). The flavor is somewhat like a chestnut.

The seeds—as with all the members of this genus and family—can be used for food. They are generally best winnowed and ground, and then cooked into a hot mush or some sort of bread or biscuit.

The leaves are also OK to eat, though you should use only the very young leaves for salads. The leaves can also be steamed or boiled and served like spinach, or added to soups, stews, egg and rice dishes, etc.

LEWIS AND CLARK
In the journals of the Lewis and Clark expedition, they found and described American bistort "in moist grounds on the quamash flats." They do not say whether or not they ate any.

MOUNTAIN SORREL
Oxyria dignya

The mountain sorrel plant with seeds PHOTO BY HAGAN

There are 4 species of *Oxyria*, and apparently only this species is found in Oregon.

Use: Edible leaves and seeds
Range: Found throughout the Cascades and Olympic Mountains in the subalpine and alpine areas
Similarity to toxic species: None
Best time: Spring and summer
Status: Sporadic
Tools needed: Collecting bag

PROPERTIES
This plant seems to prefer the harsher environment of higher elevations, never growing in massive stands, but a little here, a little there. It's relatively easy to recognize and collect a few leaves for your meal.

Closeup of the mountain sorrel seeds
PHOTO BY STEVE MATSON

This is a perennial herb with mostly basal leaves. The leaves are heart shaped to kidney shaped, about 2 inches across and on a stem that's about 3 to 4 inches long. The erect stem rises no more than 8 to 10 inches tall.

If you're familiar with the other members of this family, like dock or sheep sorrel, you'll probably notice the family resemblance. The flowers are also typical of this family, with many green-to-reddish flowers clustered on the stalk, which rises about a foot tall. There are 4 perianth segments (petals and sepals), with the outer 2 spreading. There are 6 stamens and 2 red stigmas. When the seeds mature in the fall, they will be more conspicuously red, flat, and winged like the dock seeds.

USES
Mostly found in the higher elevations, so this isn't a backyard plant. You might add some to a meal when out hiking or backpacking.

The leaves are tart, like sheep sorrel, and are great added to salads. Try them with an avocado salad. They're also good in a mixed salad. The leaves are a great addition to stews, soups, freeze-dried meals, MREs, etc.

The flavor is very much like oxalis or sour grass, so you'll be adding this to other recipes, not making dishes from it entirely. A handful of the leaves makes a tart addition to soups cooked up on the trail.

SHEEP SORREL
Rumex acetosella

View of the sheep sorrel plant

There are about 190 to 200 species of *Rumex* worldwide, with at least 17 in Oregon, not counting varieties or subvarieties.

Use: The leaves are good raw in salads and can also be added to various cooked dishes.
Range: Found in the higher elevations, often around water, and often near disturbed soils and in urban areas
Similarity to toxic species: None
Best time: Spring to early summer
Status: Can be abundant locally
Tools needed: None

PROPERTIES
Sheep sorrel is native to Europe and Asia. It is common and widespread and is recognized by its characteristic leaves, which are generally basal, lance to oblong shaped, with the base tapered to hastate or sagittate. In other words, it looks like an elongated arrowhead. When the seed stalk matures, it is brown, reminiscent of the curly dock seed stalk but much smaller.

This view of the sheep sorrel plant shows the arrowhead-shaped leaves.

A camper collects some of the tender sheep sorrel greens for dinner.

USES

Where the plant is common, you can pinch off many of the small leaves to add to salad, or even to use as the main salad ingredient. I've enjoyed sheep sorrel salads with just avocado and dressing added. The leaves are mildly sour, making a very tangy salad.

The flavor is somewhat similar to the leaves of oxalis, though not as strong. They can be effectively added raw to other foods like tostadas (in place of lettuce) or sandwiches. They add a bit of a tang when added to soups and stews, and can be very effective at livening up some MREs.

The only objection I've heard voiced about this plant is that it is so small that it takes awhile to get enough to make a difference in a dish. Still, I always pick a little when I see this one, and I notice that there are many other people who do likewise.

RECIPE

Shiyo's Garden Salad

Rinse a bowl full of young sheep sorrel leaves. Add at least 1 ripe avocado and 1 ripe tomato, both diced. Toss with some Dr. Bronner's oil and vinegar dressing. Eat it outside where the wind can blow your hair.

CURLY DOCK
Rumex crispus

BROAD-LEAFED DOCK
Rumex obtusifolius

Nyerges inspects a patch of full-size dock leaves, some of which were collected for lunch.
PHOTO BY RICK ADAMS

There are about 190 to 200 species of *Rumex* worldwide, with at least 17 in Oregon, not counting varieties or subvarieties.

Use: Young dock leaves eaten raw or cooked; seeds harvested and added to various flours; stems used like rhubarb
Range: Prefers wet areas but can be found in most environments
Similarity to toxic species: None

A view of the rosette of dock leaves

The immature seed spike, still green PHOTO BY HELEN W. NYERGES

Best time: The leaves are best gathered when young in the spring. Seeds mature in late August, and they may be available for months.
Status: Common and widespread
Tools needed: None

PROPERTIES

Curly dock is a widespread perennial invasive plant in most of Oregon. It is originally from Europe, and today is not only found in Oregon but worldwide. Though it has many good uses, it is often despised and poisoned because it not only survives well, but often takes over entire areas.

The root looks like an orange carrot, and the spring leaves arise directly from the root. The young leaves are long and linear, and curved on their margins. The leaves can be over a foot long and pointed.

As the season progresses, the flower stalk arises, and it can reach about 4 feet, even taller in ideal conditions. The seeds are formed with 3 to each unit, with a papery sheath around the seed. They are green at first and then mature to a beautiful chocolate brown.

The mature seed spike of the curly dock plant

USES

You can make meals from both the leaves and the mature seeds of curly dock. Let's start with the leaves.

Pick only the very youngest leaves for salad, the smaller ones before the plant has begun to send up its seed stalk. These will be not too tough, and the flavor will be sour, somewhat like the French sorrel. You can just rinse them, dice them, and add them to salads. I've had only these for salad, with dressing and avocado, and it was good, but only because the leaves were young.

Older leaves are best boiled like spinach, or—ideally with the midrib removed—sautéed with potatoes and onions. Or you can just add some to soup and stews. The leaves change color and darken a bit upon cooking, and the cooking softens up the tougher older leaves. But you really want to cook older leaves, as they are tougher and bitter and astringent, all of which is reduced somewhat by cooking.

I have seen the brown seed spikes sold in floral supply shops as "fall decoration," and they are very attractive. Those little seeds can be stripped off the stalks with your hands, and then rubbed between the hands to remove the wing from the seed. You don't have to be too picky here, as it can all be used. I blow off the wings and then mix the seed half-and-half with flour for pancakes, and sometimes bread. You could also toss some seed into soup to increase the protein content.

I've seen some folks go to the trouble of winnowing and then further grinding the seeds in a mill to get a fine flour. I never bother, but some folks prefer the finer flour, which is a bit more versatile than the seeds. For example, a fine flour can be mixed half-and-half with wheat, blended, and put through a pasta machine to make a curly dock seed pasta, which tastes really good.

The leaf stems are tart and sour but often make a good nibble. Young stems can be processed and used like rhubarb for pies.

This closer look at the seeds of the dock plant shows how each seed is "winged."

Curly Dock "Nori" (Vegetable Chips)

Dehydration is a neat way to make some interesting and flavorful ingredients for wild food dishes. This one is easy to do. You will just need a silicone sheet.

100 grams chopped curly dock

1 garlic clove

½ cup water

2 teaspoons soy sauce

¼ teaspoon salt

Blend all the ingredients and, using a spatula, spread on a silicone sheet.

Dehydrate at 160°F until fully dry.

—RECIPE FROM PASCAL BAUDAR

PURSLANE FAMILY (PORTULACACEAE)

The Purslane family has recently been redefined by botanists as having only the one genus, with about 100 species worldwide, and only this species found in Oregon. Many of the plants that were formerly in this family are now a part of the Miner's Lettuce family. This family was considered by Dr. Leonid Enari to be entirely safe for consumption.

PURSLANE
Portulaca oleracea

The sprawling purslane plant displays its paddle-shaped leaves.

Use: Entire aboveground plant can be eaten raw, cooked, pickled, etc.

Range: Prefers disturbed soils of gardens and rose beds; also found in the sandy areas around rivers

Similarity to toxic species: Somewhat resembles prostrate spurge. However, spurge lacks the succulence of purslane. Also, when you break the stem of spurge, a white milky sap appears.

Best time: Spring into summer

Status: Relatively common

Tools needed: None

PROPERTIES

Purslane starts appearing a bit later than most of the spring greens, typically by June or July. It is a very common annual in rose beds and gardens, though I do see it in the wild too, typically in the sandy bottoms around streams.

A view of the succulent, reddish stems of the purslane

The stems are succulent, red-colored, and round in the cross section. The stems sprawl outward from the roots, rosette-like, just lying on the ground. The leaves are paddle shaped. The little yellow flower is 5-petaled.

USES

When you chew on a fresh stem or leaf of purslane, you'll find it mildly sour and a bit crunchy. It's really a great snack, and I like it a lot in

Wild purslane growing on a sandy beach

The prostrate, sprawling purslane plant, showing the yellow flowers

salads. Just rinse to get all the dirt off, dice, add some dressing, and serve. Yes, add tomatoes and avocado if you have any.

Add it to sandwiches, tostadas, even on the edges of your chiles rellenos and huevos rancheros. I've also eaten it fried, boiled, baked (in egg dishes), and probably other ways too.

Purslane is often sold at farmers' markets, sometimes under the Spanish name *verdolago.*

It's versatile, tasty, and crisp. It really goes with anything, and it's very nutritious.

If you take the thick stems and clean off the leaves, then cut them into sections of about 4 inches, you can make purslane pickles. There are many ways to make pickles; my way is to simply fill a jar with purslane stems, add raw apple cider vinegar, and let it sit for a few weeks. (I refrigerate it.)

According to researchers, purslane is one of the richest plant sources of omega-3 fatty acids. That means not only is it good, it's good for you!

RECIPE

Purslane Salsa

2 cups chopped tomatoes

2½ cups chopped foraged purslane

¾ cup chopped onions

3 garlic cloves

1 cup apple cider vinegar

¼ cup sugar

1 large Oregon myrtle leaf

½ cup chopped cilantro and some herbs from the garden (thyme, etc.)

Salt and pepper to taste

Place all the ingredients except the cilantro and herbs in a pot, bring to a boil, and then simmer until the right consistency (light or chunky). Add the cilantro and herbs at the end, and salt and pepper to taste.

Pour into jars, close the lids, and place in the fridge. It should be good for at least a month.

—RECIPE FROM PASCAL BAUDAR

ROSE FAMILY (ROSACEAE)

The Rose family contains 110 genera and 3,000 species worldwide. At least 42 of these genera are found in Oregon.

SERVICEBERRY (a.k.a. JUNEBERRY)
Amelanchier alnifolia

A section of the serviceberry shrub with fruit PHOTO BY JOHN DOYEN

The *Amelanchier* genus consists of about 25 species, only 3 of which (and several varieties) are found in Oregon.

Use: Edible berries
Range: Most common in riparian and moist hillside areas, all the way up to alpine areas
Similarity to toxic species: None
Best time: Late summer and fall
Status: Somewhat common
Tools needed: Collecting basket

PROPERTIES

Serviceberry is a large shrub or small tree with deciduous leaves, often forming in dense thickets. There are 5 varieties of *A. alnifolia*.

A view of the
fruit of the
serviceberry
PHOTO BY LOUIS-M.
LANDRY

The twigs of this native are glabrous, and the leaf is elliptical to round, with obvious serrations, generally serrated above the middle of the leaf. The flowers are 5-petaled, white, fragrant, and in clusters of a few to many. The fruit is a pome of 2 to 5 papery segments, berrylike, generally spherical, bluish black to purple in color, with a waxy outer skin. Each fruit contains 2 seeds. The shape somewhat resembles a tiny pomegranate.

USES

The ripe fruits are good to eat raw, dried, or prepared into jams, etc. Fruits of several species of *Amelanchier* were used for food by various Native American tribes, and all members of this genus are edible. Fruits ripen in late spring and into the summer.

Native peoples ate these fruits fresh, or they dried them for later use. The ripe berries were mashed with water into a paste by the Atsugewi and then eaten fresh. Several of the western tribes were known to dry these fruits and then shape them into loaves for future use.

The berries would remain sweet when dried and could be reconstituted later when added to water. In some cases, this would be served as a sweet soup. With sugar and flour added, these fruits have been made into a pudding. The fruit can be dried, ground, and used in a pemmican mix.

STRAWBERRY
Fragaria spp.

Wild strawberry growing as a ground cover

Fragaria contains 20 species worldwide, with 3 found wild in Oregon, all native.

Use: Edible berries; leaves used for tea

Range: Can be found from the beaches up to the mountain meadows

Similarity to toxic species: None

Best time: Spring and summer

Status: Widespread

Tools needed: Collecting basket

PROPERTIES

If you've grown strawberries in your yard, you will recognize these 3 wild strawberries:

The beach strawberry (*F. chiloensis*) is found along the beaches and coastal grasslands, from California north to Alaska. Receptacle is about 10 to 20 millimeters; leaf petiole is generally 2 to 20 centimeters.

The wood strawberry (*F. vesca*) is found in partial shade in the forests throughout Oregon. Receptacle is about 5 to 10 millimeters; leaf petiole is generally 3 to 25 centimeters.

Fruit of *F. vesca* PHOTO BY DR. AMADJ TRNKOCZY

The mountain strawberry (*F. virginiana*) is found in the higher elevations in meadows and forest clearings. Receptacle is more or less about 10 millimeters; leaf petiole is generally 1 to 25 centimeters.

Their leaves are all basal, generally 3-lobed, each leaflet having fine teeth. They look just like the strawberries you grow in your garden but smaller.

Technically, the strawberry berry is an aggregate accessory fruit, meaning that the fleshy part is derived not from the plant's ovaries but from the receptacle that holds the ovaries. In other words, what we call the "fruit" (because, obviously, it looks like a fruit) is the receptacle, and all the little seeds on the outside of the "fruit" are technically referred to as achenes, actually one of the ovaries of the flower, with a seed inside it.

Though the wild strawberry prefers higher-elevation forests and clearings, it is found widely throughout the state.

Forager note: Strawberry leaf tea (made by infusion), though not strongly flavored, is popular in many circles. It is high in vitamin C and generally used as you'd use blackberry leaf or raspberry leaf tea. It's a mild diuretic and has astringent properties, and is regarded as a tonic for the female reproductive system. When made stronger, the tea is said to be good for alleviating hay fever.

The strawberry plant in flower PHOTO BY JEAN PAWEK

Wild strawberries are pretty easy to identify. When the average person sees one, especially if it's summer and the plant is in fruit, they will typically say, "Hey, look, isn't that a wild strawberry?" Strawberries are so widely known that just about everyone recognizes them when they see them, even though the wild varieties are significantly smaller than the huge ones that can be found in the markets. Cultivated strawberries can get to be about 2—even up to 3—inches long. That's huge! By contrast, a wild strawberry is between ¼ and ½ inch long. A ½-inch wild strawberry is a big one!

Though they may be smaller, the wild strawberries are typically sweeter, firmer, and tastier. Yes, it may take longer to collect them, but you'll find that it's worth it.

USES
You use these in every way that you'd use cultivated strawberries. Eat them as is, dry them, make into jams and jellies, put on top of ice cream and pancakes, etc.

The berries of the beach (or sand) strawberry were eaten by all the coastal Native people.

INDIAN PLUM
Oemleria cerasiformis

A view of the flowers and leaves PHOTO BY STEVE MATSON

There is only one species of *Oemleria*, the Indian plum, which is sometimes also called oso berry.

Use: Edible fruits
Range: Mostly found west of the Cascades, from Canada down into California. Prefers moist lowlands and stream banks, but can also be found in dry woods.
Similarity to toxic species: None
Best time: Early summer
Status: Widely distributed
Tools needed: Collecting bag or basket

The immature fruit PHOTO BY STEVE MATSON

The leaves and flowers of the Indian plum plant
PHOTO BY MATT BELOW

PROPERTIES

The Indian plum is a small tree to large shrub, loosely branched, generally about 5 to 10 feet tall. Alternately arranged leaves are long and ovate, a bit like an avocado leaf, about 3 inches long with a unique fruity aroma when crushed. Leaves are deciduous.

A dozen or so white to whitish-green, 5-petaled, drooping flowers are found on each stem; there are both male and female plants. The twig is slender, green turning to reddish brown, pith chambered, with conspicuous orange lenticles. The bark is smooth and reddish brown to dark gray in color.

The fruits begin in early spring with an orange color, and mature to a

The Indian plum flowers PHOTO BY KEIR MORSE

blue-black color. The fruit is fleshy, and there is a large flattened seed in each one. Of course, the fruits form only on the female plants.

The Indian plum fruit PHOTO BY KEIR MORSE

USES

Not everyone likes the flavor of the Indian plum, since it can be bitter and astringent. But the taste varies, and there are some foragers who regard this as one of the better-tasting wild fruits. You can eat these raw, as you'd eat any other fruits, assuming they are palatable. Try them in fruit dishes and salads. When there is a predominant bitterness to the fruits, try them cooked instead.

You can also enjoy these cooked and made into jams, jellies, and pie fillings. The cooking mellows the flavor a bit and reduces any bitterness that might be present.

The indigenous peoples of Oregon ate the fruit and made tea from the bark. Some also chewed on the small twigs, which acted as a mild anesthetic. Some said it also acted as an aphrodisiac . . . hmmm.

WILD CHERRIES
Prunus spp.

Prunus Virginiana PHOTO BY BOB KRUMM   Chokecherry blossoms PHOTO BY BOB KRUMM

There are about 400 species of *Prunus* worldwide, whose common names generally include cherry, almond, apricot, and plum. At least 15 species of *Prunus* are in Oregon, but we're only concerned with the cherries here: chokecherry (*P. virginiana*), bitter cherry (*P. emarginata*), and western chokecherry (*P. virginiana* var. *demissa*).

Use: Flesh of the fruit in jams and jellies; meat of the large seed processed into a flour
Range: Cascades, coastal ranges, riparian, urban fringes
Similarity to toxic species: In a sense, these are toxic plants. The leaves are mildly toxic—see Cautions, below. And the fruit could get you sick if you do not process it as described below.
Best time: Fruits mature around July into August.
Status: Common
Tools needed: None

PROPERTIES
One way to identify the plant is to crush the leaves, wait a few seconds, and then smell them. They will have a distinct aroma of bitter almond extract, your clue that the leaf contains "cyanide" (hydrocyanic acid).

Fruit of *Prunus virginiana* PHOTO BY LOUIS-M. LANDRY   Leaf from Prunus virginiana PHOTO BY LOUIS-M. LANDRY

The fruits are very much like cultivated cherries, except the color is darker red, almost maroon, sometimes even darker. The flesh layer can be very thin in dry years and thicker in the seasons following a good rain. Like domestic cherries, there is a thin shell and the meaty inside of the seed.

USES

The fruit of our wild cherries makes a great trail nibble. I usually see them in August when they ripen, when the trail is hot and dry, and the fruit makes a refreshing treat, if not too sour. But don't eat too many of the raw fruit or diarrhea might result.

The wild cherry also has a hint of bitterness. The fruit can be cooked off the seeds, and the pulp made into jellies, jams, and preserves. You can also make a fruit leather by laying the pulp on a cookie sheet and drying it.

In the old days the Native people enjoyed the flesh of the cherry, but they considered the seed to be the more valuable part of the fruit. The seeds were shelled and the inside meat was cooked to reduce the cyanide. The cooked seeds, once ground into mush or meal, were then used to make a sweet bread product or added (like acorns) to stews as a gravy or thickening agent.

The bark was boiled by Native people and used as a cough and sore throat remedy, as well as for treating diarrhea and headaches.

CAUTIONS

If you crush the leaf, it will impart a sweet aroma like the bitter almond extract used in cooking. That's the telltale aroma of cyanide, so don't use the leaf for tea.

LEWIS AND CLARK

On June 11, 1805, Meriwether Lewis became sick and wrote, "I was taken with such violent pain in the intestens that I was unable to partake of the feast of marrow-bones. . . . I directed a parsel of the small twigs [of chokecherry] to be geathered striped of their leaves, cut into pieces of about 2 Inches in length and boiled in water until a strong black decoction of an astringent bitter tast was produced; at sunset I took a point [pint] of this decoction and abut an hour after repeated the dze. By 10 in the evening I was entirely relieved from pain and in fact every symptom of the disorder forsook me; my fever abated, a gentle perspiration was produced and I had a comfortable and refreshing nights rest."

A colander of shelled cherry seeds

Vickie Chiu shows a bag of cherry seeds and a bowl of shelled cherry seeds, which will be boiled and cooked with acorns.

WILD ROSE
Rosa spp.

Wild rose hips

There are about 100 species of *Rosa* worldwide, which hybridize freely. At least 12 species can be found in the wild in Oregon, not including varieties, and not including the large array of cultivated roses grown in gardens.

Use: Fruits eaten raw or cooked and made into jam or tea; wood useful for arrow shafts
Range: Typically riparian but found in many areas; cultivated roses are common in urban areas.
Similarity to toxic species: None (but be wary of eating fruit or flower from roses where various commercial fertilizers and insecticides have been used).
Best time: Fruits mature in summer
Status: Common
Tools needed: Clippers, possibly gloves

PROPERTIES
Wild roses are more common than most people think. They are typically found in wet areas, though this is not a fast rule. The wild rose flowers are 5-petaled, not the multiple-petaled flowers that you find on hybridized roses. After the flowers mature and fade, the fruit develops, often called the "hip," which is usually smaller than a grape. The fruit is bright orange.

The leaves are oddly divided into 3, 5, or 7 petals, and the stalks are covered in thorns. If you've ever had rose bushes in your yard, you have a pretty good idea of what the wild rose looks like.

The wild rose is often in dense thickets. If it gets cut down, or after a burn, there will be many straight shoots in the new growth.

USES

For food, we have the flower and the fruits. The flowers have long been used to make "rose water" and could also be used to make a mild-flavored infusion. The petals make a flavorful, colorful, and nutritious garnish to soups and salads.

A wild rose flower

The fruits—commonly called "hips"—are one of the richest sources of vitamin C. The fruits can be eaten fresh, but you should first split them open and scrape out the more fibrous insides. They are typically a bit fibrous, with a hint of bitterness. The fruits are more commonly cooked into a tea or made into jellies.

Some "old-school" archers consider the rose shaft one of the finest woods to use for making arrows, assuming you cut the new straight shoots. You need to then ream the shaft through a rock with a hole in it to remove the thorns.

CAUTIONS

Before you eat the petals or fruit, make sure the plants have not been sprayed with any pesticides.

The shoots of wild rose were dried, cleaned of thorns, and used as arrow shafts by indigenous peoples.

BLACKBERRY
Rubus spp.

Blackberry in flower

There are about 400 to 750 species of *Rubus* worldwide, including at least 14 in Oregon (not including varieties). These include blackberry, raspberry, and salmonberry, a.k.a. thimbleberry (*R. parviflorus*).

Use: Berries used for juices, jams, and desserts or dried; leaves used for medicine
Range: Riparian and many other areas where sufficient water is supplied
Similarity to toxic species: Somewhat resembles poison oak, though poison oak lacks the thorns.
Best time: Fruits mature in summer.
Status: Very common
Tools needed: None, but clippers can help.

PROPERTIES
Most people instantly recognize the shape of the blackberry because they've seen it in supermarkets or in backyard gardens. The aggregate fruit is a collection of sweet drupelets, with the fruit separating from the flower stalk to form a somewhat hollow, thimble-like shape.

The sprawling vine of the blackberry PHOTO BY HELEN WONG

USES

The blackberry is fairly universally recognized, and everyone who sees the ripe ones ventures out to eat them. I've picked them in the foothills and mountains and along roadsides. The key is to avoid the thorns and to make sure they are not immature and tart. If the fruit is black, soft, and easily picked—it's ripe! You can eat them right away, or pick a bunch and mash them for a pancake, biscuit, or cake topping. Even better, sprinkle them over a bowl of vanilla ice cream. (Yes, we know that chocolate ice cream is better for you, but the flavor of blackberries clashes a bit with chocolate.)

Ripe and unripe fruit of the blackberry

The flowers of the Himalayan blackberry, *Rubus bifrons* PHOTO BY LILY JANE TSONG

Thimbleberry PHOTO BY JEAN PAWEK

Salmonberry PHOTO BY VERNON SMITH

You could also make a conserve, a jam, a jelly, a pie filling, or a juice. It's a very versatile berry. And though I rarely have ripe blackberries around long enough to dry them, they can be dried in any food dehydrator and will keep for quite a while. The dried fruits can then be eaten as is or reconstituted for juices or desserts.

An infusion of the leaves has long been used among Native Americans for diarrhea and childbirth pains.

LEWIS AND CLARK

Lewis and Clark collected a sample of thimbleberry near The Dalles on April 15, 1806. (The site was a major Native American trading center for at least 10,000 years.) Frederick Pursh described the sample as "a shrub of which the natives eat the young Sprout without kooking."

NIGHTSHADE FAMILY (SOLANACEAE)

There are 75 genera of the Nightshade family and 3,000 species worldwide. Eight genera are found in Oregon. Many are toxic, and many are good foods.

BLACK NIGHTSHADE
Solanum nigrum

A view of the nightshade plant with flowers and immature fruits

There are approximately 1,500 species of *Solanum* in the world, with 13 found in Oregon. *S. americanum* is a native, and *S. nigrum* is introduced. You are more likely to find *S. nigrum* in Oregon, and it's very difficult to distinguish from *S. americanum*.

Use: Fruits eaten when ripe, raw or cooked
Range: Disturbed soils, urban areas, chaparral
Similarity to toxic species: According to many, this is a toxic species, meaning don't eat the raw green fruits, and don't eat the leaves raw. Sickness is likely in either case. There is also a slight resemblance to jimsonweed, which is in the same family.
Best time: Summer
Status: Somewhat common
Tools needed: None

The fruit of nightshade

PROPERTIES

The very young plant much resembles lamb's quarter, except that the nightshade doesn't have an erect stem. Rather, it's more widely branched. Also, though the individual leaves of both nightshade and lamb's quarter are quite similar, the nightshade lacks the mealy coating of the lamb's quarter and lacks the often-noticeable red in the axil of the leaf that is common in lamb's quarter.

The 5-petaled white to lavender flower is a very typical nightshade family flower, resembling the flowers of garden tomatoes. The fruits begin as tiny BB-size green fruits, and by August ripen into purplish-black little "tomatoes." We've eaten the listed *Solanums* with no problems.

The nightshade plant showing mature fruit PHOTO BY DR. AMADEJ TRNKOCZY

USES

The fruit of this plant seems to peak around August, when the plant can be prolifically in fruit if the season's rain and heat have been just right. Regardless, I have found ripe fruit of the black nightshade during every month.

You don't want to eat these fruits raw while they are still green, as this could result in a stomachache and minor sickness. They should first be boiled, fried, or otherwise cooked. I will, on the other hand, try a few of the dark purple ripe fruits if I see them while hiking. I like the fresh tartness. It's very much like eating a tomato, but a bit spicier. They are great added to salads—just like adding tomatoes!

But just like tomatoes, there are many other ways to enjoy the ripe western nightshade fruit.

My friend Drew Devereux shared with me his experiments of smashing these fruits and adding them to pizza dough, as you'd use garden tomatoes. They taste like regular tomatoes but turn nearly black when cooked.

Urban farmer Julie Balaa examines two plants that can be easily confused for each other in the young stages: black nightshade on the left, and green lambs quarter (*Chenopodium murale*) on the right.

They are good added to soup too. You don't need to cut or slice them, since they are so small. Just toss them into your soup or stew.

Also, just like sun-dried tomatoes with their unique flavor, you can let western nightshade berries dry in the sun (or in your oven or food dryer) and then eat as is or reconstitute later into various recipes. Though it isn't absolutely necessary, I find that they dry quicker if you gently smash them first—such as on the cookie sheet that you'll be drying them on.

CAUTIONS

While there are other ripe nightshade fruits that could be eaten, we don't advise you eat any but the one listed above. Also, do not eat the green berries. Only eat the fully ripe, dark purple berries. Otherwise, sickness could result. Green berries should only be consumed if boiled, fried, or otherwise cooked. Anyone with a tomato sensitivity, or sensitivity to other members of this family (e.g., eggplant, chilies, peppers), should not consume these fruits.

NETTLE FAMILY (URTICACEAE)

The Nettle family includes 50 genera and 700 species worldwide. Two of those genera are found Oregon.

STINGING NETTLE
Urtica dioica

A young nettle plant

A patch of young nettle plants

There are 45 species of *Urtica*, only 2 (not counting varieties) of which are found in Oregon.

Use: Leaves used for food and for tea; stalks made into fiber
Range: Riparian, urban fields, edges of farms, disturbed soils, etc.
Similarity to toxic species: While nettles itself is regarded as a mechanical toxin by some botanists, it is safe to eat the cooked greens.
Best time: Collect the greens in the spring.
Status: Common
Tools needed: Gloves, snippers

PROPERTIES

This perennial generally sends up a single stalk in the winter or spring that can reach around 5 feet tall if undisturbed. The leaves are oblong, with toothed margins, and tapering to a point. Both the leaves and the stalks are covered with bristles that cause a stinging irritation when you brush against them.

Chopping tender nettle leaves to add to soup

Cooking nettle greens on the campfire

An open-air mesh dryer used to dry nettle

Though it's a European native, you can find it all over Oregon, along streams in the wilderness and in fields and backyards.

USES

The young, tender leaf tips of nettle are the best to use, though you could also collect just the leaves later in the season (the stems get too tough). These tender tops can be steamed and boiled, which removes the sting of the nettles. They are tasty as a spinach-like dish, alone or served with butter or cheese or other topping. Also try the water from the boiling—it's delicious!

We've also made delicious stews and soups, which began by boiling the nettle tops. Then we quickly added diced potatoes, some red onions, and other greens. You can also add some miso powder. Cook until tender and then serve, perhaps with Braggs Liquid Amino Acid added for some great flavor and nutrition.

RECIPE

Pascal's Stinging Nettle Hot Sauce

I created this hot sauce through experimentation and really enjoyed it. It has a mild "wild" flavor and was really liked by those who tasted it. It's extremely simple to make. This is a basic recipe, but you can add some of your favorite flavors and ingredients, such as Italian herb, bay leaves, etc. As for supplies, you'll need latex gloves, a blender (or go primitive with a knife and a *molcajete*), jars or bottles, and a metal pot.

5 ounces jalapeño peppers, stemmed and chopped with seeds (make sure they're not too hot, though)

1 ounce serrano peppers

5 ounces fresh nettle leaves (or young nettles)

Juice from 2 limes

6 garlic cloves

3½ cups apple cider vinegar

1 teaspoon kosher or pickling salt

1 cup water or white wine (I used white wine in my original recipe)

Blend all the ingredients until smooth. Strain for a thinner sauce, or keep it as is for a thicker sauce. Transfer to jars and cover. Refrigerate at least 2 weeks, then enjoy!

—RECIPE FROM PASCAL BAUDAR

This is a vitamin-rich plant, so you'll be getting your medicine when you eat it.

FIBER

The stalks of the mature nettle plants can be gently pounded, washed, and then twined into serviceable cordage.

CAUTIONS

As you will probably learn from personal experience, you get "stung" when you brush up against nettle. This is due to the formic acid within each "needle," which causes a skin irritation. So be careful when you gather nettle greens by wearing gloves or other protection. And if you do get the nettle rash, you can treat it with fresh aloe vera gel or with the freshly crushed leaves of plants such as chickweed or curly dock.

Forager note: Nettles are an undervalued medicine, and herbalists speak highly of the many uses for nettle tea. I have found that drinking nettle tea in the spring helps to alleviate the symptoms of pollen allergies.

VIOLET FAMILY (VIOLACEAE)

There are 23 genera of this family and about 830 species, around 500 of which are *Viola*, the only genera found in Oregon.

VIOLET
Viola spp.

Violets (*V. adunca*) in the wild PHOTO BY JEAN PAWEK

There are at least 28 species of *Viola* in Oregon, not including varieties.

Use: Edible leaves and flowers
Range: Widespread, growing in most environments in Oregon. You can find them in the prairies, foothills, urban areas, subalpine zones, etc.
Similarity to toxic species: None
Best time: Spring
Status: Common
Tools needed: Just a bag for collecting

PROPERTIES
These are commonly planted as garden plants, and they are hardy. They will spread by their roots and appear to naturalize in areas where they were once cultivated. In fact, they are very easy to cultivate if you want some nearby for your meals.

Wild *Viola odorata* PHOTO BY JEAN PAWEK

Though there is great variety in size and minor leaf characteristics, they all have heart-shaped leaves, usually on a long stem of a few inches. The flowers are white, purple, blue, and even yellow, though the cultivated ones are purple or blue.

USES

When I learned that you can eat violets, I began by collecting the heart-shaped leaves from neighbors' yards as I walked home from school. As I came to recognize them, I noticed that they were very common on the edges of people's yards, probably just going wild from an original planting. I'd pick a few leaves here and few there, and when I got home, I'd cook them up with a little water and season them with just butter. I loved them!

I have collected the tender leaves of spring, washed them and diced them, and added them to omelettes. I've even tried some diced and added to ramen soup. They are very versatile, not strongly flavored, and can be added to many dishes.

The leaves are also edible raw, and they add their mild flavor to salads. Some people find the leaves a bit strong or tough in salads, but it's really a matter of personal preference.

The flowers are often used to make jellies, or added to jellies, as well used in various dessert items. I have had a gelatin product that someone else made using the purple flowers, and I thought it was very tasty.

Monocots

These have just 1 cotyledon, which emerges from the sprouted seed. Leaf veins are generally parallel from the base or midrib, and flower parts are generally in 3s—with 3 petals and 3 identically appearing sepals.

ONION (OR GARLIC) FAMILY (ALLIACEAE)

There are 13 genera and 750 to 800 species of the Onion family worldwide.

WILD ONIONS, ET AL.
Allium spp.

Flowering wild onion PHOTO BY HELEN W. NYERGES

There are about 700 species of *Allium* worldwide, with at least 29 in Oregon. Most are natives.

Use: Bulbs and greens eaten raw or cooked. However, I strongly advise the reader to leave the bulbs in the ground and only pick the greens for food.

Range: Can be found in just about every type of environment in Oregon

Similarity to toxic species: See Cautions

Best time: The leaves and flowers are most noticeable in the spring and early summer.

Status: Though in certain areas you will not find wild onions, they can be common locally.

Tools needed: None

PROPERTIES

Wild onions go by many names including ramps, wild garlic, and leeks. In general, they look like small "green onions" from the market, though many are inconspicuous when not in flower.

The entire wild onion plant
PHOTO BY RICK ADAMS

There is a small underground bulb, and the leaves are green and hollow. The flower stalk tends to be a bit more fibrous than the leaves. There appear to be 6 petals of the same color, but in fact there are 3 sepals underneath the 3 identical petals, giving the appearance of a 6-petaled flower. The expedient field key to identifying a wild onion is the unmistakable aroma. If you don't have that aroma, you shouldn't use the plant because similar-appearing members of the Lily family could be toxic or poisonous.

Wild onions can be found all over the United States in a broad diversity of eco-types. In Oregon we find a lot in the eastern desert regions and in higher-elevation meadows and fields. We notice them mostly when they flower, because otherwise they appear very much like grass.

USES

When you find wild onions, you'll be tempted to pull up the plant so you can eat the bulb. That's what you probably do in your own garden, but that's not the only way you can use these. Generally, I only pick the green leaves for consumption. If there are a lot of them, I might take some of the bulbs to eat, and break up the cluster and replant some. The reason that I generally only eat the greens is that I've seen some patches of wild onions disappear entirely due to foragers uprooting the whole plant.

So, while the wild onion bulbs can be used in any of the myriad ways in which you're used to eating garlic, onions, chives, leeks, et al., you'll still get most of the flavor and most of the nutritional benefits by eating only the leaves. I pinch off a few leaves here, a few there, and add them to salads. Diced, they're great in soups, stews, egg dishes, and stir-fries. And if you ever have to live off MREs, you can spice them up, and add to their nutritional value, by adding wild onion greens.

All tender parts of wild onions are edible, above and below ground. Generally, the older flower stalks become fibrous and unpalatable. Otherwise, the bulbs and leaves are all used raw or cooked. Simply remove any outer fibrous layers of the plant, rinse, and then use in any of the ways you'd use green onions or chives.

Wild onions can be added to salads, used as the base for a soup, cooked alone as a "spinach," chopped and mixed into eggs, cooked as a side to fish, and used to enhance countless other recipes. Wild onions share many of the healthful benefits of garlic, and they improve any urban or wilderness meal. Backpackers who are relying on dried trail rations will certainly enjoy the sustenance of wild onions. Many American Indians heavily relied on wild onions and regarded them as a staple, not just a condiment.

Excellent health benefits are associated with eating any members of this group. Some of these benefits include lowering of cholesterol levels, prevention of flu, and reduction of high blood pressure. Used externally, the crushed green leaves can be applied directly to wounds to prevent infection.

CAUTIONS

Never forget that some members of the Lily family with bulbs are deadly poisonous if eaten. Wild onions used to be classified in the Lily family because their characteristics are so similar. Make absolutely certain that you have correctly identified any wild onions that you intend to eat. You should check the floral characteristics to be certain that there are 3 sepals and 3 petals. Then, you must detect an obvious onion aroma. If there is no onion aroma, do not eat the plant. Though there are a few true onions that lack the onion aroma, it is imperative that you have absolutely identified those nonaromatic species as safe before you prepare them for food.

RUSH FAMILY (JUNCACEAE)

The Rush family has 7 genera and 440 species worldwide. In Oregon it is represented by only 2 genera.

RUSH
Juncus textilis, et al.

A view of the long hollow leaves of *Juncus* while seeding

A view of the base of the *Juncus* plants

There are 315 species of *Juncus* worldwide. In Oregon over 50 species (not counting varieties) have been recorded.

Use: Tender white growth at base of shoots edible raw or cooked; seeds cooked in pastry or porridge. Leaves have long been used in the manufacture of baskets, mats, sandals, boats, and other useful crafts.
Range: Riparian and coastal areas
Similarity to toxic species: In the young stages, there is a superficial resemblance to members of the Lily family, some of which are toxic.
Best time: Spring for the shoots; fall for the seeds
Status: Common locally
Tools needed: None

PROPERTIES

When seeing *Juncus* for the first time, many folks think it's a type of grass or cattail, or they might say "reed." Yes, it has a grasslike appearance, but there are some important differences that put this plant into a different family.

The leaves are long, grasslike, and hollow from top to bottom. There are various lengths of *Juncus*, and *J. textilis* can be found in thick patches up to 5 or 6 feet tall. The leaves are round in the cross section. The flowers are inconspicuous, bits of seed on the end of long stems, tassel-like, and are formed near the top of each leaf, generally off to one side.

Like many grasses and the cattails, these spread with an underground system of rhizomes. They are typically found in association with wet areas, such as a spring or river, though they are not necessarily right in the water, such as you'd find with watercress.

USES

Though this plant and its close relatives are thought of as great weaving and fiber plants, they provide at least two good food sources as well.

In the fall there will be a small tassel of seeds on the top portion of the rushes. If you're there at the right time, you can put a bag under the tassel and shake out the seeds. These seeds are then used in the two ways in which most grains can be used: mixed in with pastry products or as a cooked cereal.

In the spring when you can gently pull up the long leaves, you will notice that the bottom of the plant is white and tender. There's not a lot of food here, but it's good, and you can get a decent amount in a short period of time. You can eat them raw on the spot, or save them to add to salads, stir-fries, or soups.

The tender white base of a *Juncus* shoot

The long linear leaves of the *Juncus* plant are ideal for weaving.

Danielle Del Vale weaves a traditional basket from the *Juncus* leaves.

Harvesting the shoots seems to make the rush patches grow better, but you still shouldn't just pick these for the tender base and then discard the rest, because you really only get a nibble from each shoot. The upper part of the plant—the long leaves—are great for making traditional baskets. So if you're going to eat some of the young bases, you should really collect the shoots and use them for weaving, or give them to someone who makes baskets. Unless, of course, you're lost and starving, which is a wholly different situation. . . .

Forager note: The leaves, properly prepared, are ideal for many of the traditional basketry done by Native peoples. One of the best "how-to" descriptions of this is found in Paul Campbell's book *Survival Skills of Native California*.

ASPARAGUS FAMILY (ASPARAGACEAE)

There are 3 genera in this relatively new family, created out of the Lily family (Liliaceae). Asparagaceae contains about 320 species, the majority of which (about 300) are a part of the Asparagus genus. There are 12 genera of this family in Oregon.

WILD ASPARAGUS
Asparagus officinalis

A bundle of collected asparagus spears

Of the approximately 300 species of *Asparagus*, this is the only one recorded in Oregon.

Use: Young shoots eaten

Range: Not common west of the Cascades; more common in eastern Oregon

Similarity to toxic species: See Cautions

Best time: Spring

Status: Common in areas

Tools needed: Knife, bag

When you find the mature asparagus plant, as depicted here, you can return next spring to that same spot to search for the young emerging shoots. PHOTO BY DR. AMADEJ TRNKOCZY

The mature asparagus plant with red berries PHOTO BY JIM ROBERTSON

PROPERTIES

The edible part of this European native is the first spring shoots, which are iden-tical to the cultivated plant. Have you ever seen an asparagus spear in the pro-duce store or at a farmers' market? Now you know what wild asparagus looks like! The wild asparagus can be an escapee from gardens and farms and would not be uncommon along a road or trail.

As the asparagus shoot continues to grow, numerous stems grow out of the main shoot. As these stems and their ferny leaves mature, the overall appearance of the plant begins to resemble a 3- to 5-foot-tall ferny bush. As the shoots grow, they become intricately branched, giving the entire plant a ferny appearance. Eventually the plant develops ¼-inch-long, bell-like green flowers that are fol-lowed by small berries, dark green at first, then maturing to red.

USES

Wild and cultivated asparagus are more or less identical. The wild shoots can be used in all the ways in which you'd use store-bought asparagus. They can be

A man harvests the asparagus spears. PHOTO VIA GETTY IMAGES, 121759797

steamed or boiled and served with butter, cheese, or whatever. They can be made into soup or added to soups and stews, and even eaten raw in salads.

The plant is inedible once it has grown to the point of being highly branched.

CAUTIONS

Eating raw asparagus shoots and the small red berries causes a mild dermatitis reaction in some individuals. Do not eat the red berries of the maturing plant. Consume only the newly emerging shoots.

CAMAS
Camassia quamash

A view of the flower of the edible blue camas
PHOTO BY JEAN PAWEK

The flower of the edible blue camas PHOTO BY ZOYA AKULOVA

There are three species of *Camassia* in Oregon, and botanists have defined four subspecies of *C. quamash*. This was formerly classified in the Lily family (Liliaceae), and sometimes classified in the Century Plant family (Agavaceae).

Use: The bulbs are the traditional food of this plant.

Range: Though once widespread, urban development has wiped out many of the traditional sites. Found in wet and well-drained soils. Common in the grasslands and valleys. Tends to grow in wet soils, rarely in dry soils.

Similarity to toxic species: Death camas; see notes under Cautions

Best time: Gather the bulbs in late spring and early summer.

Status: Certainly less common than in the past; making a comeback as a garden plant

Tools needed: A trowel or shovel

PROPERTIES

Traditionally a part of the Lily family, this perennial lily-like plant consists of a deep bulb from which grasslike leaves arise. The leaves are all basal and flat, up to an inch wide, and anywhere from 5 to 15 inches in length. The flower stalks may be up to 2 feet tall. The purple flowers are over an inch wide, consisting of 3 sepals and 3 petals that both look alike, so it appears to have 6 purple petals. There are 6 stamens and a 3-parted pistil. As the flower matures, the fruit enlarges, which is a 3-lobed dry capsule about an inch long, full of the black seeds.

The camas bulb
PHOTO BY KYLE CHAMBERLAIN

USES

Camas bulbs—up to an inch in diameter—were once one of the most important foods for the indigenous people of this region. There are still places where you can find them abundantly. When you find them and you want to eat them, dig up the largest and rebury the smaller ones. To be safe, especially if you are just beginning, only dig the bulbs of those plants that are in flower.

You don't eat these raw, or they will cause upset stomach and severe flatulence. They need to be baked for about a day or more. Traditionally, these were baked from one to three days in a fire pit. A hole is dug, lined with rocks, and a fire is built and burned for at least 3 hours. Layers of grass and edible vegetation are laid down, and then a layer of clean cotton can be laid down to keep the bulbs clean. The bulbs are then covered with a layer of more edible vegetation and covered with soil. You can dig these out in 12 hours or so, but up to three days is better.

John Kallas of Wild Food Adventures found that by cooking the bulbs for 9 hours in a pressure cooker at 257 degrees, he produced a sweet-tasting bulb. If you don't have a pressure cooker, you can simply try cooking on a stove top, though it takes about 24 hours of cooking to make the bulbs digestible and tasty. The longer the better—just don't let your pan go dry.

The bulbs can be eaten once processed. They can be dried and powdered and then used in making breads, biscuits, gravy, etc.

In sum, don't eat these raw, and make absolutely certain that you have the right bulb.

LEWIS AND CLARK

The journals have more information about this plant than any other plant the explorers encountered. On September 20, 1805, Clark described how they were searching for food and came upon an Indian village where they were given buffalo meat, dried berries, and salmon, and some round roots. He described the roots as "much like an onion, which they call quamash the Bread or Cake is called Pas-she-co Sweet, of this they make bread & Supe they also gave us the bread made of this root all of which we eate heartily."

Clark goes on to explain how the camas bulbs were cooked in a traditional fire pit, but doesn't say how long they were cooked. He writes, "I find myself verry unwell all the evening from eateing the fish & roots too freely." Other members of the party also had intestinal pains that lasted for days. The camas roots were probably not cooked long enough.

Once steamed in the pits, Lewis wrote on June 11, 1806, how the camas bulbs were further processed by the Indians. He stated that the roots were dried in the sun, where they become black and "of a sweet and agreeable flavor." He added, "If the design is to make bread or cakes of the roots they undergo a second process . . . reduced to the consistency of dough and then rolled [into] cakes of eight or ten lbs are returned to the sweat." Once the dough is removed from the fire pit the second time, they are made into little cakes about ½- to ¾-inch thick and dried in the sun or by the fire. According to Lewis, these cakes "will keep sound for a great length of time. This bread or the dryed roots are frequently eaten alone by the natives with further preparation, and when they have them in abundance they form an ingredient in almost every dish they prepare. This root is palateable but disagrees with me in every shape I have used it."

CAUTIONS

There are bulbs that resemble, and may be related to, the edible camas, which can kill you. Make sure you have positively identified any bulbs before you eat them. This might take several seasons until you know what the living plant looks like.

Please read about death camas, below, whose territory might overlap with the edible camas. See the photos; the flowers of each have the same Lily family configuration, but the edible one is blue, and the toxic one is greenish white. Though death appears to be rare after eating the death camas, it can still cause serious sickness.

DEATH CAMAS
Zigadenus elegans and *Z. venenosus*

There is also a plant known as death camas, which closely resembles the edible camas. Death camas typically grows in drier soils, and its flower is greenish white, often described as yellow. However, the territories of both can overlap.

It's easy to tell these plants apart when they are in flower, but there are reports of indigenous people getting very sick when the death camas bulbs were accidentally dug up and included with the edible bulbs. (Death is apparently somewhat rare if you eat the death camas, but you'll get seriously ill.)

The overall plant—leaves and bulbs—of the death camas is very similar to the edible camas, though the flowers are smaller and greenish white. In fact, there are at least 20 species of the death camas, mostly in the *Zigadenus* genus, though botanists have been doing a lot of reclassifying of these species.

A view of the toxic death camas PHOTO BY JEAN PAWEK

Closer view of the flowers of the death camas PHOTO BY JEAN PAWEK

Bottom line: The edible camas has the blue flower and can fade to a pale color, somewhat resembling the death camas. If you're uncertain, don't eat it! The death camas will never have the bright-blue flower of the edible camas, so if you only collect when the plant is in flower, you'll be OK.

GRASS FAMILY (POACEAE)

There are 650 to 900 genera worldwide, with about 10,550 species. A massive group! There are so many species that the family is divided into 5 or 6 major categories, depending on the botanist. (Some botanists are joiners, some are splitters, and the splitters seem to be getting the upper hand.) In Oregon there are over 80 genera and hundreds of species.

The Grass family has the "greatest economic importance of any family," according to botanist Mary Barkworth, citing wheat, rice, maize, millet, sorghum, sugarcane, forage crops, weeds, thatching, weaving, and building materials.

A patch of wild oats

A wild oat plant

Use: Leaves for food (sprouts, juiced, etc.); seeds for flour or meal; some are obviously better than others.

Range: Grasses are truly found "everywhere."

Similarity to toxic species: See Cautions

Best time: Somewhat varies depending on what grass we're talking about, but generally spring for the greens and summer to fall for seed.

Status: Very common

Tools needed: None

PROPERTIES

The large plant family Poaceae (formerly Gramineae) is characterized by mostly herbaceous but sometimes woody plants with hollow and jointed stems, narrow

Indian rice grass

Angelo Cervera gathers the seed of the Indian rice grass.

sheathing leaves, petal-less flowers borne in spikelets, and fruit in the form of seedlike grain. It includes bamboo, sugarcane, numerous grasses, and cereal grains such as barley, corn, oats, rice, rye, and wheat.

Grasses are generally herbaceous. They can be little annuals to giant bamboos. The stems are generally round and hollow, with swollen nodes. The leaves are alternate, generally narrow linear sheathing leaves, with petal-less flowers formed in spikelets and fruit in the form of seedlike grain. The flowering and seed structures are rather diverse, ranging from the sticky seeds of the foxtail grasses that get caught in your socks, to the open clusters of sorghum, to such seeds as rice and wheat and the cobs of corn. Indeed, whole books have been written describing the diversity of this large family.

USES

The edibility of the wild grasses, generically, can be summed up in two categories: the young leaves and the seeds.

You may have had some of the leaf when you went to a health food store and ordered "wheatgrass juice." That's perhaps one of the best ways to eat various grass leaves—juice them. You can purchase an electric juicer or a hand-crank juicer. I have juiced various wild grass leaves and found the flavor to be quite diverse. Some have the flavor of wheatgrass juice and are good added to drinks or to soup broth. Some are very different, almost like seaweed, and these are typically better in soup.

Simple hand-winnowing can be used to separate grass seed from the chaff (or outer covering).

However you do it, get the grasses as young as possible. They are most nutritious at this stage and are less fibrous. You will discover that grasses contain *a lot* of fiber once you start to crank a hand juicer, and watch as the green liquid gold comes out one end and the strands of fiber come out the other end. If you don't have a juicer, you could eat the very young grass leaves in salads or cooked soups, though you may find yourself chewing and chewing and spitting out fiber.

The seeds of all grasses are theoretically edible, though harvesting them is very difficult—if not next to impossible—in some cases. Some grass seeds are easy to collect by hand. They are then winnowed. Some are very easy to winnow off the outer chaff; some are more problematic. I have put "foxtail" grass seeds in a small metal strainer and passed them through a fire in order to burn off the outer covering. Though I was left with a little seed, I found this method less fruitful than simply locating other grasses with more readily harvestable seeds.

The seeds you gather for food should be mature and have no foreign growths on them. Then you either grind them into flour for pastry products (bread, biscuits, etc.) or cook into mush like a cereal.

With thousands of species worldwide on every landmass, and large numbers found in Oregon, the grasses are a group that we should get to know better. Not only are they arguably more important than trees in holding the earth together—their combined root systems are vast—but they are a valuable food source, assuming you are there at the right time to harvest the seed or leaf.

CAUTIONS

Be aware that many substances are added to lawns and golf courses to keep the grasses green and bug-free. Those grasses could get you sick, so harvest with caution and common sense. Also, make sure that any seed you harvest is mature and free of any mold—mold will typically give the grain a color, such as green, white, or black. Do not eat moldy grass seeds.

CATTAIL FAMILY (TYPHACEAE)

The Cattail family contains 2 genera and about 32 species worldwide.

CATTAIL
Typha spp.

The mature cattail spike, which has turned brown due to the color of the mature seeds. This is often referred to as the "hot dog on a stick."

The *Typha* genus contains about 15 species worldwide, with at least 2 of those species in Oregon, *T. latifolia* and *T. augustifolia*.

Use: Food (inner rhizome, young white shoots, green female spike, yellow male pollen); leaves excellent for fiber crafts where high tensile strength is not required
Range: Wetlands
Similarity to toxic species: None
Best time: Generally, the shoots and spikes are best collected in the spring. The rhizome could be collected at any time.
Status: Common in wetlands
Tools needed: Clippers, possibly a trowel

PROPERTIES

Everyone everywhere knows cattail, right? Think of the cattail as that grassy plant in the swamp that looks like a hot dog on a stick. Always growing in slow-moving waters or the edges of streams, their long flat leaves grow up to 6 feet tall and sometimes taller. The newly emerging leaves arise from the underground horizontal rhizomes. When the plants flower in spring, the flower spike is green, with yellowish pollen at the top. As it matures, the green spike ripens to a brown color, creating the familiar fall decoration: the hot dog on the stick. The brown that we see is actually all the individual seeds.

USES

Euell Gibbons used to refer to cattails as the "supermarket of the swamps," which is a good description of this versatile plant. There are at least four good food sources from the cattail, which I'll list in order of my preference.

In the spring the plant sends up its green shoots. If you get to them before they get stiff and before the flower spike has started, you can tug

The young green flowering spike of the cattail PHOTO BY RICK ADAMS

David Martinez inspects the mature cattail spikes and tall linear leaves.

them up and the shoot breaks off from the rhizome. You then cut the lower foot or so and peel off the green layers. The inner white layer is eaten raw or cooked. It looks like a green onion, but the flavor is like cucumber.

The spike is the lower part of the flower spike, technically the female part of the flower. You find the spike in spring, when it's entirely green and tender. Though you could eat it raw, it's far better boiled. Cook it like corn on the cob, butter it, and eat it like corn on the cob. Guess what? It even tastes like corn on the cob. You could also scrape off the green edible portion from the woody core and add to stews or stir-fries, or even shape into patties (with egg or flour added) and cook like burgers.

The pollen is the fine yellow material that you can shake out of the flower spikes. The flower spike is divided into two sections: the lower female part, which can be eaten like corn on the cob, and directly on top, the less substantial male section, which produced the fine yellow pollen. If you're in the swamp at the right time, typically April or May, you can shake lots of pollen into a bag and then strain it (to remove twigs and bugs) and use it in any pastry product.

The rhizome is also a good starchy food. You get into the mud and pull out the long horizontal roots. Wash them, and then peel off the soft outer layer. You could just chew on the inner part of the rhizome if you need the energy from the natural sugar, or you could process it a bit. One method of processing involves mashing or grinding up the inner rhizome, and then putting it into a jar of water.

The inner white portions of the young shoots are edible in salads or cooked dishes. This is the so-called "Cossack asparagus."

As the water settles, the pure starch will be on the bottom, and the fiber will be floating on the top, so you can easily scoop it out and discard it. The starch is then used in soups or in pastry and bread products.

UTILITY

Aside from cooking, the long green leaves have a long history of being used for various woven products that will not be under tension, such as baskets, sandals, and hats, and even for the outer layers of the dwellings utilized by many of the West Coast Native Americans.

And when that cattail spike matures to a chocolate-brown color, it can be broken open, and it all turns to an insulating fluff. Each tiny seed is actually connected to a bit of fluff that aids in the transportation of that seed to greener grass on the other side. You can use that fluff to stop the bleeding of a minor wound, as an alternative to down when stuffing a sleeping bag or coat, and as a fantastic fire starter!

To use as a fire starter, simply spark into the pile of fluff with your ferrocerium rod (or other sparking device), and stand back! The straight stems of the flowering spikes make excellent chopsticks and, though not ideal, can be used for arrow shafts.

OTHER EDIBLES

Do you have a favorite Oregon wild food that isn't listed here? There are many other plants such as the clovers, dead nettle, yampa, arrowheads, various Lomatiums, bitterroot, balsamroot, other ferns, and more. In many cases, we treated the members of a genus collectively, such as all the kin of the blackberries, which includes all members of the *Rubus* genus, including the huckleberries. This is why we encourage you to take classes in the field where you live, and study the other references we give.

Please read each description of each family carefully, since many of the members of certain families are entirely or mostly edible, with certain considerations. This includes such families as the Mustard family, Onion family, Cactus family, Chicory Tribe of the Sunflower family, and others.

We're well aware that there are many more wild plants that can be eaten, but remember, it was our intent to include those plants that are the most widespread throughout Oregon and readily recognizable, and those that would make a significant contribution to your day-to-day meals. We also wanted to have plants that represented most of the biological zones in the state. Additionally, we don't want you eating any endangered or rare species, so they've not been included. This book was compiled based on what we ascertained were the plants that you are most likely to be eating from the wild most of the time.

As you continue your study of ethnobotany, you will discover that there are many more wild plants that could be used for food. Some are marginal, and some just aren't that great.

In fact, there are many other wild Oregon greens that I have eaten, even some that I never found described in a wild-food or ethnobotany book. Yes, they are "edible," but after trying them, I realized why ancient people never used them, or only used them when nothing else was available. That's the real meaning of the term *starvation food*—you'd only eat it if you actually had next to nothing else to eat.

Yes, there are many wild animals and ocean life that could be used for food—fish, snakes, lizards, birds, small mammals, insects—but this book is about the plants.

THE STUDY OF MYCOLOGY
Some of the books in the Foraging series include a few common mushrooms in the mix of wild plants that you can bring into your kitchen. After much thought, I have chosen not to include them here, for various reasons. For one thing, there already exists some very good field mycology books written by trained mycologists.

While there are many readily recognized edible fungi, I never ate wild mushrooms on my own until I'd spent about two years of active study and actual "dirt-time" field work. If you want to begin using wild mushrooms for food, I am of the opinion that you should first plan on spending as much time as you devote to at least a four-unit college course for at least two semesters, preferably more.

There are many reasons for this. For the most part, you cannot go back day after day to the same mushroom to study it in detail and watch its growth cycle. Mushrooms come suddenly and decompose just as rapidly. They are not like the oak tree that will be there every day.

Not all mushrooms have been identified, and even less is known about the edibility of most species. And in their attempt to further clarify the relationships of mushrooms, mycologists occasionally rename a mushroom. The changes in Latin names causes initial confusion to wild-food foragers. And though I regularly eat about two dozen wild mushrooms, I am always humbled by the occasional newspaper article describing how a lifelong mycologist ate the wrong mushroom and died!

There are many books and videos today that are exclusively devoted to giving you an understanding of how mushrooms grow, their classification, and how to accurately identify those that are edible. Even better than books and videos are classes and clubs where you go into the field and see the mushrooms for yourself.

RESOURCES

For those of you who are seriously interested in identifying and eating wild mushrooms, I encourage you to enroll in a mycology course at a local college, or join a local mushroom group. There are many such groups nationwide, including several in the state of Oregon. (If you cannot find one, contact me and I will try to find one close to you.) You owe it to your longevity to take the time to learn about mushrooms directly with someone who has already done so. You need to learn about the different types of fungi and why they grow where and when they grow. You need to see these mushrooms in the field, and see how they develop throughout their usually short growing period.

Perhaps the greatest problem with a book is that the author will naturally want to show only the best photos of the mushrooms or plants. Of course! But not all the specimens of a given type will look exactly like the photo in the book. Nor does the book have the space to show you all the variations from new growth to seeding plant.

GETTING STARTED

Exploring the Fascinating World of Wild Plants

During the many field trips and classes that I have conducted since 1974, I have often been asked how I got interested in the subject of edible wild plants. More importantly, someone will want to know how they should go about learning to identify and use wild foods in the safest and quickest way possible.

Though I had very little prior knowledge of ethnobotany when my interest began (about age 12 or 13), I began to seek out local botanists from whom I could learn. I also took every class on this subject and related subjects that I could, both in high school and college. In addition, I spent a lot of time in the fields, foothills, mountains, desert, and at the beach looking at plants and collecting little samples to take back to my growing body of mentors.

All this took time, and I learned the plants one by one, by the primary method that I still recommend: Show the plant to an expert for identification, or go into the field with an expert so the plant can be identified. Then, once you've identified the plant, you can do all your research in books such as this one, and—assuming it's an edible plant—you can begin to experiment with all the ways you can eat it.

I learned some of the very common widespread plants first, and I would carefully clip samples, take them home, and try them in salad or as cooked greens. Some of the very first plants I began to eat were mustard, miner's lettuce, purslane, and watercress, as these were very common and easy to collect. Once I learned the identity of another edible plant, I would try it in various recipes over the course of the next several weeks, until I felt I "knew" that plant well, and my interests moved on to learning a new plant.

There was no quickie "rule of thumb" for knowing what I could or could not eat. There were no lazy-man rules of looking for red in the plant, the color of the berries, or whether the plant left a bad taste in my mouth. There was simply the effort to discover, to learn one new plant at a time, to utilize that plant in the kitchen, and to watch that plant throughout the growing season so I got to know what it looked like as a sprout, growing up, maturing, flowering, going to seed, and dying. Through observation, I would be able to recognize these common floral beings even if I was driving by in a car at a high speed.

So that is what you should do: Seek out a mentor or mentors, study with them, take them plants, get to know the plants, and continue forever with your learning. Then, use your books, videos, and Internet references as a backup to your firsthand interaction with the plant.

Where I grew up, I lived close to the local mountain range, so hiking in the hills was my after-school or weekend choice of recreation. I began to backpack and carry a heavy load, and I found it unpleasant—one of those things that you just had to put up with if you wanted to backpack. But then I met a man who talked about how he learned about foods that the Indians of Northern California used in the old days. He mentioned a few specific plants, and something clicked in my brain, and I knew that was a skill I had to learn. When I returned from my backpacking trip, I began to research ethnobotany at the local library and museums, and I sought out teachers and mentors.

The fact that I was always interested in the ways of Native Americans, and in practical survival skills, helped immensely. Plus, my mother often told us of the hard times she experienced growing up on the family farm in Ohio. I knew that knowledge of wild foods was an important skill that too many of us had lost.

By January of 1974, I began to lead wild-food outings that were organized by WTI, a nonprofit organization focused entirely on education in all aspects of survival. I led half-day walks where we'd go into a small area, identify and collect plants, and make a salad and maybe soup and tea on the spot. I became an active member of the local Mycological Association and made rapid progress in learning about how to identify and use mushrooms. And I continued to take specialized classes and field trips in botany, biology, taxonomy, and ethnobotany. I spent many hours in the classroom and lab of Dr. Leonid Enari, who was the chief botanist at the Los Angeles County Arboretum in Arcadia. He was a walking encyclopedia, and he also took the time to mentor me, to answer all my plant questions, and to help me with sections of my first wild-food book.

Today there are many more learning avenues than were available for me, such as the Internet. Most of what I learned, I learned the hard way, in spite of the fact that I had many teachers along the way. So, when I teach I attempt to provide a way that my students can save time and can learn more rapidly. In short, I try to provide an ideal learning environment that I wish I'd had.

It is to your advantage to completely disregard any of the "rules of thumb" you've ever been taught about plant identification—you know, the shortcuts for determining whether or not a plant is edible, such as: If a plant has a milky sap, it is not edible. If a plant causes an irritation in the mouth when you eat a little, it is not safe to eat. If the animals eat the plants or berries, they are safe to eat. If the berries are white, they are poisonous. If the berries are black or blue, they are safe to eat. And on and on. Disregard all these shortcuts since—although often based on some fact—they all have exceptions. As Spock would say, "Insufficient data." There are no shortcuts to what is necessary: You must study, and you will need field experience.

If there is any sort of "shortcut" to the study of plants, it is to learn to recognize plant families, and learn to know which families are entirely safe for consumption. Beyond that, you must learn plants one by one for absolute safety.

I strongly suggest that you take at least a college course in botany (preferably taxonomy) so you get to know how botanists designate plant families. This will enable you to look at my list of safe families, and then use the books written by botanists of the flora of your area so you can check to see which plants in your area belong to any of the completely safe families. After a while, this will come easy. Eventually, you'll look at a plant and examine it, and you'll know which family it likely belongs to.

Get a botanical flora book written for your area and study it. In Oregon there are a few that are used by botanists. See "Useful References" below.

Do your own fieldwork, ideally with someone who already knows the plants. Gradually, you will eventually be using more and more wild plants for food and medicine, and perhaps for soap, fiber, fire, and more. There will be no such thing as a "weed." You will cringe whenever you see the television commercials in the spring for such noxious products as Roundup that promise to kill every dandelion on your property.

When you discover that we have ruined the earth in the name of "modern agriculture," which produces inferior "food," you will understand the meaning of the phrase "We have met the enemy, and he is us."

TEST YOUR KNOWLEDGE OF PLANTS

Here is a simple test that I use in my classes. Take the test for plants and mushrooms and see how you do.

1) ❏ True. ❏ False. Berries that glisten are poisonous.

2) ❏ True. ❏ False. White berries are all poisonous.

3) ❏ True. ❏ False. All blue and black berries are edible.

4) ❏ True. ❏ False. If uncertain about the edibility of berries, watch to see if the animals eat them. If the animals eat the berries, the berries are good for human consumption.

5) Would you follow the advice below? State yes or no, and give your reasons.
    According to *Food in the Wilderness* authors George Martin and Robert Scott, "If you do not recognize a food as edible, chew a mouthful and keep it in the mouth. If it is very sharp, bitter, or distasteful, do not swallow it. If it tastes good, swallow only a little of the juice. Wait for about eight hours. If you have suffered no nausea, stomach or intestinal pains, repeat the same experiment swallowing a little more of the juice. Again, wait for eight hours. If there are no harmful results, it probably is safe for you to eat. (This test does not apply to mushrooms.)"

6) ❏ True. ❏ False. "A great number of wilderness plants are edible but generally they have very little food value." [Martin and Scott, ibid.]

7) ❏ True. ❏ False. Bitter plants are poisonous.

8) ❏ True. ❏ False. Plants that exude a milky sap when cut are all poisonous.

9) ❏ True. ❏ False. Plants that cause stinging or irritation on the skin are all unsafe for consumption.

10) The illustration to the right is the typical flower formation for all members of the Mustard family. Write out the formula:
___ petal(s); ___ sepal(s);
___ stamen(s); ___ pistil(s).

PISTIL   STAMENS
← PETALS
← SEPALS

11) Of what value is it to be able to identify the Mustard family?

12) ❏ True. ❏ False. Mustard (used on hot dogs) is made by grinding up the yellow flowers of the mustard plant.

13) ❐ True. ❐ False. Yucca, century plant, and prickly pear are all members of the Cactus family.

14) ❐ True. ❐ False. There are no poisonous cacti.

15) ❐ True. ❐ False. Plants that resemble parsley, carrots, and fennel are all in the Carrot (or Parsley) family and are thus all safe to eat.

16 ❐ True. ❐ False. Only 17 species of acorns are edible. The rest are toxic.

17) To consume acorns, the tannic acid must first be removed. Why?

18) If you are eating no meat or dairy products (during a survival situation, for example), how is it possible to get complete protein from plants alone?

19) ❐ True. ❐ False. There are no toxic grasses.

20) ❐ True. ❐ False. Seaweeds are unsafe survival foods.

21) ❐ True. ❐ False. All plants that have the appearance of a green onion and have the typical onion aroma can be safely eaten.

22) List all of the plant families (or groups) from this lesson which we've identified as entirely or primarily nontoxic.

ANSWERS

1. False. Insufficient data.

2. False. Though mostly true, there are exceptions such as white strawberry, white mulberry, and others. Don't eat any berry unless you know its identity, and you know it to be edible.

3. False. Mostly true, but there are some exceptions. Don't eat any berry unless you've identified it as an edible berry.

4. False, for several reasons. Certain animals are able to consume plants that would cause sickness or death in a human. Also, animals do occasionally die from eating poisonous plants—especially during times of drought. Also, just because you watched the animal eat a plant doesn't mean the animal didn't get sick later!

5. Very bad advice, even though this has been repeated endlessly in "survival manuals" and magazine articles. Since food is rarely your top "survival priority," this is potentially dangerous advice.

6. False. To verify that this is not so, look at *Composition of Foods*, which is published by the US Department of Agriculture. In many cases, wild foods are far more nutritious than common domesticated foods.

7. False. Insufficient data. Many bitter plants are rendered edible and palatable simply by cooking or boiling.

8. False. Though you can't eat any of the euphorbias, many others (like dandelion, lettuce, milkweed, sow thistle) exude a milky sap. Forget about such "shortcuts." Get to know the individual plants.

9. False. Many edible plants have stickers or thorns that must first be removed or cooked away, such as nettles, cacti, etc.

10. Mustard flowers are composed of:
    4 sepals (one under each petal)
    4 petals (the colorful part of the flower)
    1 pistil (in the very center of flower, the female part of the flower)
    6 stamens; 4 are tall and 2 are short. (The 6 stamens surround the pistil.)

11. There are no poisonous members of the Mustard family.

12. False. The mustard condiment is made by grinding the seeds. Yellow is typically from food coloring.

13. False. Only the prickly pear is a cactus.

14. True, but you must know what is and is not a cactus. There are some very bitter narcotic cacti, which you would not eat due to unpalatability. Also, some euphorbias closely resemble cacti and will cause sickness if eaten. Euphorbias exude a milky sap when cut; cacti do not. Any fleshy, palatable part of true cacti can be eaten.

15. False. The Carrot (or Parsley) family contains both good foods and deadly poisons. Never eat any wild plant resembling parsley unless you have identified that specific plant as an edible species.

16. False. All acorns can be consumed once shelled and leached of their tannic acid.

17. Tannic acid is bitter.

18. Combine the seeds from grasses with the seeds from legumes. This generally produces a complete protein. For details, see *Diet for a Small Planet* by Frances Moore Lappé. *Note:* When speaking of "complete protein," we're mostly concerned about the 9 amino acids that the body does not manufacture. Acorns actually contain all of the 9 essential amino acids, though in small amounts. Prickly pear cactus pads contain all but one of the 9 essential amino acids, again, in small amounts.

Traditional Diets That Combine Legumes and Grass Seeds to Make a Complete Protein

Loosely based upon "Summary of Complementary Protein Relationships," Chart X in *Diet for a Small Planet* by Lappé

	Legumes	Grasses
Asian diet	Soy (miso, tofu, etc.)	Rice
Mexican diet	Beans (black beans, etc.)	Corn (tortillas)
Middle East diet	Garbanzos	Wheat
Southern United States	Black-eyed peas	Grits
Starving student	Peanut butter	Wheat bread
Others to consider	Mesquite, palo verde, peas, carob, etc.	Millet, rye, oats, various wild grasses, etc.

19. True. However, be certain that the seeds are mature and have no mold-like growth on them.

20. False. Seaweeds are excellent. Make certain they've not been rotting on the beach, and don't collect near any sewage-treatment facilities.

21. True. But be sure you have an onion!

22. All members of the Mustard family, all palatable cacti, all acorns, all cattails, grasses, seaweeds, onions. There are many other "safe" families, but you will need to do a bit of botanical study in order to identify those families. Begin by reading the descriptions of each family in this book. Also consider getting *Botany in a Day* by Tom Elpel.

THE DOZEN EASIEST-TO-RECOGNIZE, MOST WIDESPREAD, MOST VERSATILE WILD FOODS OF OREGON

In the mid-1970s I began to investigate the edibility of whole plant families and found that there were quite a few entire families that are safe to eat, given a few considerations in each case. Some of these families are difficult to recognize unless you are a trained botanist. Still, in this book I have described many of the entirely safe families. My original research on this was done with Dr. Leonid Enari, who was one of my teachers and the chief botanist at the Los Angeles County Arboretum in Arcadia, California.

The chart below was the idea of my friend Jay Watkins, who long urged me to produce a simple handout on the dozen most common edible plants that everyone should know. Granted, there are many more than a dozen, but as Jay and I discussed this idea, I decided to focus on 12 plants that could be found not just anywhere in the United States, but in most locales throughout the world. The result was the accompanying chart, which is largely self-explanatory.

This chart assumes that you already know these plants, since its purpose is not identification. Anyone who has studied wild foods for a few years is probably already familiar with all these plants. However, not everyone is aware that these plants are found worldwide.

This overview should help both beginners as well as specialists. It is merely a simple comparative chart, which could be expanded to many, many pages. It is deliberately kept short and simple.

	Description	Parts Used	Food Uses	Preparation	Benefits	Where Found	When Found
Acorns	The fruit of the oak tree	Acorns (nuts)	Flour, pickles, mush	Leach out tannic acid first, then grind	Similar to potatoes	Mountains, valleys	Fall
Cactus	Succulent desert plants of various shapes	Tender parts; fruit	Salad; cooked vegetable; omelette; dessert; drinks	1. Carefully remove spines 2. Dice or slice as needed	Pads said to be good for diabetics; fruits rich in sugar	Dry desertlike environments; Mediterranean zones	Young green pads in spring and summer; fruit in summer and fall
Cattail	Reedlike plants; fruit looks like hot dog on stick	1. Pollen 2. Green flower spike 3. Tender shoots 4. Rhizome	1. Flour 2. Cooked vegetable 3. Salads 4. Flour	1. Shake out pollen 2. Boil 3. Remove outer green fibrous parts 4. Remove outer parts, crush	Widespread, versatile	Wet areas, e.g., roadside ditches, marshes	Spring through fall
Chickweed	Weak-stemmed, opposite leaves, 5-petaled flower	Entire tender plant	Salads, tea	Clip, rinse, and add dressing, or make infusion	Good diuretic	Common and widespread when moisture is present	Spring and summer
Dandelion	Low plant, toothed leaves, conspicuous yellow flower	1. Roots 2. Leaves	1. Cooked vegetable, coffee-like beverage 2. Salads, cooked vegetable	1. Clean and cook; or dry, roast, grind 2. Clean and make desired dish	Richest source of beta carotene; very high in vitamin A	Common in lawns and fields	Best harvested in spring
Dock	Long leaves with wavy margins	1. Leaves 2. Stems 3. Seeds	1. Salads, cooked vegetable 2. Pie 3. Flour	1. Clean 2. Use like rhubarb 3. Winnow seeds	Richer in vitamin C than oranges	Common in fields and near water	Spring through fall
Grasses	Many widespread varieties	1. Seeds 2. Leaves	1. Flour, mush 2. Salads, juiced, cooked vegetable	1. Harvest and winnow 2. Harvest, clean, and chop	1. Easy to store 2. Rich in many nutrients	Common in all environments	1. Fall 2. Spring
Lamb's Quarter	Triangular leaves with toothed margins, mealy surface	1. Leaves and tender stems 2. Seeds	1. Salads, soups, omelettes, cooked 2. Bread, mush	1. Harvest and clean 2. Winnow	Rich in vitamin A and calcium	Likes disturbed rich soils	Spring through fall
Mustard	Variable leaves with large terminal lobes; 4-petaled flowers	Leaves, seeds, some roots	Salads, cooked dishes, seasoning	Gather, clean, cut as needed	Said to help prevent cancer	Common in fields and many environments	Spring through fall
Onions	Grasslike appearance; flowers with 3 petals, 3 sepals	Leaves, bulbs	Seasoning, salads, soups, vegetable dishes	Clean and remove tough outer leaves	Good for reducing high blood pressure and high cholesterol level	Some varieties found in all environments	Spring
Purslane	Low-growing succulent, paddle-shaped leaves	All tender portions	Salads, sautéed, pickled, soups, vegetable dishes	Rinse off any soil	Richest source of omega-3 fatty acids	Common in parks, gardens, disturbed soils	Summer
Seaweeds	Marine algae of many shapes and colors	Entire plant	Depends on seaweed: salads, soups, stews, broth	Use dried, raw, or cooked, depending on species	Excellent source of iodine; great salt substitute	Oceans	Year-round

Latin names: Acorns = *Quercus* spp.; Cattail = *Typha* spp.; Chickweed = *Stellaria media*; Dandelion = *Taraxacum officinale*; Dock = *Rumex crispus*; Grasses = *Poaceae* (Grass family); Lamb's quarter = *Chenopodium album*, Mustard = *Brassica* spp. / Mustard family = Brassicaceae; Onions = *Allium* spp.; Purslane = *Portulaca oleracea*; Seaweeds = brown, red, and green marine algae (Phaeophyceae, Rhodophyceae, Chlorophyceae)

STAFF OF LIFE: BEST WILD-FOOD BREAD SOURCES

Baking of bread goes back to the most ancient cultures on the earth, back when mankind discovered that you could grind up the seeds of grasses, add a few other ingredients, let it rise, and bake it. There are countless variations, of course, but bread was once so nutritious that it was called the "staff of life."

Most likely, the discovery of bread predated agriculture, since the earth was full of wild grasses and a broad assortment of roots and seeds that could be baked into nutritious loaves. Most grains store well for a long time, which allowed people the time to pursue culture, inner growth, technology, etc. The development of civilizations and the development of agriculture go hand in hand. And bread was right there from the beginning.

Today, we are at another extreme of a very long road of human development. We started with the struggle for survival, and with the surplus of the land allowing us the time to develop more fully in all aspects. That good bread from the earth was heavy, rich, and extremely nutritious. It was a vitamin-and-mineral tablet.

We produced so much grain that the United States called itself "the bread-basket of the world." And this massive volume resulted in losses in the fields from insects and loss due to spoilage. Thus came the so-called Green Revolution where chemical fertilizers replaced time-honored fertilizers such as animal manures, straw and hay, compost, bone meal, and other such natural substances that the modern farmer was too busy and too modern to use. Crops increased while the nutritional values dropped. And though this is a gross oversimplification, bread from the supermarket is no longer the staff of life.

The mineral content of the once-rich soils of the United States has steadily declined. Producers process and refine "white flour" and then add certain minerals back into the bread dough. We sacrificed quality since we thought it would bring us security, and we knew it would bring big bucks. Now, the great irony is that we lost the quality of the food, of the soil, and ultimately we are no more secure than ever before. Why? Because a soil rich in natural organic matter can withstand floods and droughts and the ravages of insects. It is the folly of man who causes the droughts and plagues of modern times.

There is much—very much—that we need to learn about "modern agriculture," or "agribiz" as it is more appropriately called. We should not put our heads into the sand, ostrich-like, and pretend the problem does not exist.

Personal solutions are many. Grow your own garden. Learn about wild foods, and use them daily. By using common wild plants, you can actually create a nutritious bread comparable to the breads your ancestors ate. The easiest way to get started is to make flour from these wild seeds and mix that flour half-and-half with your conventional flours, such as wheat. You'll end up with a more flavorful, more nutritious bread, pancake, or pastry product.

Once you begin to use your local wild grains, you'll be amazed how tasty, how abundant, and how versatile these wild foods are.

The accompanying chart is by no means complete. It is a general guideline to show you what is available over widespread areas. However, there are quite a few plants of limited range that produce abundant seeds or other parts that are suitable in bread-making. In most cases, you should consult any of the many wild-food cookbooks available for details on using each of these wild grains.

Note that "Grass" is a huge category, since it actually includes many of our domestic grains such as wheat, corn, rye, barley, etc. Though some of the seeds listed in this chart can be eaten raw, most require some processing before you can eat them. Acorns must be soaked or boiled to get rid of all the bitter tannic acid. The seed from amaranth, dock, and lamb's quarter can get somewhat bitter and astringent as it gets older, and is improved by cooking.

By rediscovering the wealth of wild plants that are found throughout this country, we can bring bread back to its status as the staff of life.

RECIPE

Beginner Wild Bread Recipe

1 cup whole wheat flour

1 cup wild flour of your choice

3 teaspoons baking powder

3 tablespoons honey

1 egg

1 cup milk

3 tablespoons oil

Salt to taste, if desired

Mix all the ingredients well and bake in oiled bread pans for about 45 minutes at 250°F or in your solar oven until done.

Beginner Pancake Recipe

Follow the above recipe, adding extra milk or water so you have pancake batter consistency. Make pancakes as normal.

"Wild Bread" Chart

	Part Used	How Processed	Where Found	Palatability	Ability to Store
Acorns	Shelled acorns	Leach acorns of tannic acid by soaking or boiling, and grind into meal	Worldwide; ripens in fall	Good, if fully leached	Excellent
Amaranth	Seeds	Collect and winnow seeds	Worldwide as a weed of disturbed soils	Good	Very good
Cactus	Seeds	Mash ripe fruits, and pour through colander to extract seed	Throughout US, through most common in Mediterranean climates worldwide	Good	Good
Cattail	Pollen and rhizome	Shake the top of cattail spikes into bag to collect pollen; mash peeled rhizome and separate out fiber	Worldwide in wet and marshy areas	Very good	Good
Dock	Seeds	Collect brown seeds in fall, rub to remove "wings," and winnow	Worldwide in wet areas and disturbed soils	Acceptable	Very good
Grass—most species	Seeds	Generally, simply collect and winnow; difficulty depends on species	Worldwide; some found in nearly every environment	Generally very good	Very good to excellent
Lamb's Quarter	Seeds	Collect when leaves on plant are dry, rub between hands and winnow	Worldwide in disturbed soils and farm soils	Acceptable to good	Very good

Note: This chart is intended only as a general guideline to compare sources for "wild bread" ingredients. There may be many other wild plants which can be used for bread. Also, never eat any wild plant that you have not positively identified as an edible species.

Latin names: Acorns = *Quercus* spp.; Amaranth = *Amaranthus* spp.; Cactus = primarily *Opuntia* spp. and other Cactaceae; Cattail = *Typha* spp.; Dock = *Rumex crispus*; Grass = Poaceae; Lamb's quarter = *Chenopodium album*

SWEET TOOTH: BEST WILD-FOOD SUGARS AND DESSERTS

When people speak of "sugar" today, they are almost always talking about the highly refined nutritionless white substance made from sugarcane or sugar beets. Unfortunately, modern sugar is a foodless food. It is the "cocaine" of modern man's dinner plate. It is not good for the body, and it offer no nutrients whatsoever. But this has not always been so.

Just a few generations ago, it was common for people to make their own sugars. Every culture had their favorite sources for their sugars, depending on what was found in the wild or what was grown in that particular location. In most cases, they simply collected, dried, and ground up sugar-rich fruits. Most such fruits will naturally crystallize with time, and then could be further ground. The advantage of these sugars over "white cane sugar" is that these sugars had their own individual flavors, and they contained many valuable minerals.

Some sugars are quite simple to "produce," such as honey. The main obstacles are to find a way to house the bees—something modern beekeepers do quite well—and keep from getting stung. And tapping maple trees (and several other trees) was so simple that even the North American Indians did it. They simply cut narrow slashes into the tree, inserted hollow tubes made from elder branches, and collected the sap in whatever containers they had. Raw maple sap is usually boiled down to get a syrup of desired consistency and sugar content. Sometimes you boil off about 40 gallons of water for each gallon of syrup. You do *not* do this indoors.

People have always sought ways to make foods more flavorful, and sugar is certainly useful in that regard. But sugar is also valuable as a preservative. Both sugar and salt help to preserve foods and keep them from spoiling. This was especially important in the past when there was no electricity or refrigerators.

It's amazing how fast a modern culture forgets things. Probably not one in a thousand urbanites knows these simple details about sugar. Our culture has sunk to such ignorance in this matter that we somehow believe that the only choice is between white sugar, the pink container, or the blue container. Rather than produce nutritious sugars as we had in the past, the trend is to produce high-tech sweet substances that not only have no nutrients but have no calories either, as does white sugar. The wonders of science never cease!

For those of you who want to try making sugar, the accompanying chart gives you some ideas as to what is available. Currants and gooseberries were very popular among American Indians not as a sweetener but as a preservative. They ground up their jerky and added ground-up currants or gooseberries, and the result was pemmican.

Though many of the wild berries described in the chart have been used as sweeteners for other foods, most of them are good foods in their own right and have long been used to make such things as drinks, pies, jams, custard, and a variety of dessert items. Details for these can be found in many of the wild-food cookbooks available.

Here's one recipe, which can be used with all of the sugars in the chart except manzanita. This is because manzanita is not a fleshy berry, so they won't cook up like the others.

RECIPE

Northwest Brickle

½ gallon ripe madrone berries

Water to cover berries

½ cup honey

Approximately ⅓ cup biscuit mix

Begin by gently cooking the washed berries. When they are cooked, add the honey and stir. After the mixture thickens, stir in the biscuit mix little by little. The mix will be very thick when it is ready to serve.

This makes a heavy, sweet dessert. In the old days, what wasn't eaten would be put into a bread pan and baked until dry so it would store. It would then last a long time until reconstituted. The dried shape looked like a brick, which is the source of the name.

"Wild Sugar" Chart

	Part Used	How Processed	Where Found	Sweetness/Palatability	Ability to Store
Apples, Wild (including crab apples)	Whole fruit	Use fresh, or slice, dry, and grind to flour	Entire United States	Very good; collect when ripe	Very good
Berries (blackberries, raspberries, thimbleberries)	Whole fruit	Use fresh, or dry and grind	Entire United States	Excellent	Very good
Currants	Whole fruit	Use fresh, or dry and store	Entire United States	Good	Very good
Elder	Whole fruit	Can use fresh if cooked first, or dry and store	Entire United States	Contains sugar but tart	Good
Gooseberries	Whole fruit	Remove spiny layer, then use fresh or dry	Entire United States	Good	Very good
Grapes, Wild	Whole fruit	Use fresh, or dry	Most of the United States	Sometimes tart; collect ripe fruit	Very good
Manzanita	Whole fruit	Dry and grind entire fruit	Southwestern United States	A bit tart; used like aspic	Good
Maple	Sap	Cut bark on tree and capture sap; use fresh; crystallizes naturally	Entire United States, but best flow where there is snow	Excellent	Excellent
Prickly Pear Cactus	Fruit	Remove stickers, use inner pulp fresh or dried, with or without seed	Entire United States, but most common in Southwest	Excellent	Good

Note: Many sugars are found in nature, usually in the fruits. Honey is a traditional sugar, made indirectly from plant nectars. Other traditional sugars include dried and powdered dates, dried pomegranate juice, and beets. This chart compares a few wild sugar sources that are the most widespread throughout North America. There are many plants that are either marginal sugar sources or available in very limited locations. Never use any wild plant for sugar or food until you have positively identified it as an edible plant.

Latin names: Apples, wild = *Malus* spp.; Berries = *Rubus* spp.; Elder = *Sambucus* spp.; Gooseberries = *Ribes* spp.; Grapes, wild = *Vitis* spp.; Manzanita = *Arctostaphylos* spp.; Maple = *Acer* spp.; Prickly pear cactus = *Opuntia* spp.

LEARN THE FAMILIES

A Guide to the (Relatively) Easily Recognized Plant Families That Are Nontoxic and Primarily Edible

Learning each and every plant you plan to consume is certainly the best way to proceed with the study of edible wild plants. Nevertheless, studying the edible families should not be considered a shortcut approach, since this method still necessitates careful observation of all the floral (and other) characteristics. Be absolutely certain that you've identified a given plant as a member of one of these families before sampling any part of it.

There are many other families of plants that are for the most part safe to consume. When I compiled this list with my mentor, botanist Dr. Leonid Enari of the L.A. County Arboretum in Arcadia, California, we included those groups that are the most abundant, widespread, easily recognized, and the most palatable.

I suggest that you begin by reading the description of each family. Then try to actually observe the examples listed or other examples. By doing so, you'll begin to see and feel the similarities of all the members of each group listed. To expand your perspective, get a botany book of the flora for your particular area so you can read the botanist's description of each family. Also, in your local book of flora, there should be a list of all the members of each particular family that are known to be found in your area. Call a botanist at a local college or arboretum to find which book of flora is used in your area.

A great reference in this regard is Thomas Elpel's *Botany in a Day*, published by HOPS, Box 691, Pony, MT 59747.

The family examples listed here are some of the easiest families to recognize, but this list is by no means complete. Hopefully, you'll be able to observe as many of the examples listed as possible.

I greatly appreciate and extend thanks to Dr. Leonid Enari, who assisted me with this section.

The nomenclature here conforms with *The Jepson Manual, Vascular Plants of California* (University of California, Berkeley: 2012).

AMARANTH FAMILY (AMARANTHACEAE)

These are annual herbaceous weeds or shrubs, with leaves that are simple and entire and either alternate or opposite. The small, inconspicuous flowers are perfect or unisexual, and they are congested in terminal spikes or axillary clusters. Sepals are usually dry, thin, and membranous. No petals are present. The fruit can be a fleshy or membranous thin-walled, one-seed body that is either indehiscent, irregularly dehiscent, or circumscissile (which means that the top of the fruit separates in a circular line, much like the lid of a pillbox). The seeds are mostly black and shiny, and they mature about the time the spikes begin to fade and dry to a tan color. There are 40 genera and about 500 species worldwide.

EXAMPLES
Forty knot (*Achyranthes repens*), giant amaranth (*Amaranthus hypochondriacus*), love-lies-bleeding (*A. hybridus*), pigweed (*A. retroflexus*), tumbleweed (*A. albus*), etc.

USES
The young leaves can be eaten raw or cooked. The older leaves should be cooked since they become bitter with age. The abundant seeds can be easily harvested, winnowed, and used as a flour substitute or extender.

CAUTIONS
None.

CACTUS FAMILY (CACTACEAE)

Cactus plants are perennial succulents, herbaceous, or woody. There are believed to be as many as 2,000 species worldwide. The stems are columnar, globose, or flattened and are technically leafless in most varieties. (The pads are not considered leaves.) Branches, spines, and flowers develop in the raised areas on the stems, called areoles. The flowers have both stamens and pistils, and the flowers are sessile (stalkless). The sepals and petals are numerous and intergrading with one another, overlapping in several rows, and the bases merge together. Stamens are numerous. There is 1 pistil with 2 or more stigmas. Seeds are numerous.

EXAMPLES
Barrel cactus (*Ferocactus* spp.), hedgehog cactus (*Echinocactus* spp.), *Mammillaria* spp., prickly pear cacti (*Opuntia* spp.) including beavertail, pancake pear, Indian fig saguaro (*Carnegiea gigantea*), etc.

USES

All the cactus flesh and fruits can be eaten if they are sufficiently tender, readily available, and palatable. Most of the young cactus pads, once peeled, can be eaten raw. Most cacti, assuming they are not too woody, can be eaten. In some cases, cooking will improve the flavor and texture, thereby improving the palatability. The fruits are edible raw or cooked, once peeled of their outer skin.

CAUTIONS

Be very careful when collecting cactus. Take special precautions to protect your hands from both the spines and the tiny hairlike glochids at the base of each spine. Be sure to remove all the spines before consuming cactus. Woody parts are not used, and some parts may be very bitter, in which case, cooking may improve the flavor. A small number of relatively scarce cacti, including peyote and desert rock, are extremely bitter and, if eaten in sufficient amounts, can cause a narcotic or hallucinatory effect, often in addition to vomiting. Some *Euphorbia* spp., which resemble but are not cacti, exude a thick milky juice when cut. *Do not eat* Euphorbias since they are poisonous.

CATTAIL FAMILY (TYPHACEAE)

The cattail family consists of just cattails. By some accounts, there are up to 15 species worldwide. They are all aquatic with the familiar "hot dog on a stick" flower spike.

(See the main text under "Cattail" for uses and cautions.)

CHICORY TRIBE OF THE SUNFLOWER FAMILY (ASTERACEAE)

The sunflower family is characterized by the typical sunflower-like or daisy-like flower head (that is, having both ray and disk flowers on each head). They can be annual or perennial herbs. The sunflower family is one of the largest plant families, divided by botanists into 11 or more distinct groups called "tribes."

One of these tribes is the Chicory Tribe, characterized by being herbs with alternate or basal leaves and milky juice. The flowers, clustered in heads, are all perfect. Each ray flower is 5-toothed at its apex, an easy-to-make observation. The Chicory Tribe is Group 8 in *The Jepson Manual*.

EXAMPLES

Chicory (*Cichoreum* spp.), dandelion (*Taraxacum officinale*), hawkweed (*Hieracium* spp.), *Malacothrix* spp., mountain dandelion (*Agoseris* spp.), sow thistle (*Sonchus* spp.), wild and cultivated lettuce (*Lactuca* spp.), etc.

USES

When young, many of these herbs can be included in salads or used as the main salad ingredient. They quickly become bitter as they get older and are then best as cooked greens. The roots of some species are also worth digging up to use like parsnips or to dry, grind, and percolate into a noncaffeine beverage, as with dandelion and chicory.

CAUTIONS

Some members are quite bitter, and some are too fibrous to eat when older.

FERNS (POLYPODIACEAE)

The fronds of ferns are often finely divided, borne on stalks arising from creeping rootstocks. The spore-bearing cases (called "sori") are found on the backs or margins of the leaves, commonly in lines or in dots. Worldwide, there are believed to be as many as 6,000 species divided into about 150 genera.

EXAMPLES

Bracken (*Pteridium* spp.), cliff brake (*Pellaea* spp.), and maidenhair (*Adiantum* spp.).

USES

The young, uncurling growing tips are edible and taste nutty. They can be served steamed and covered with butter or mixed into various cooked vegetable dishes.

CAUTIONS

It is best to cook all fiddleheads if you plan to eat any quantity of them, since some may be mildly toxic when raw. Also, don't eat any of the mature fern fronds; some are safe, but you'd need to know each fern's individual characteristics.

Researchers have identified a substance called ptaquiloside, a known carcinogen, in bracken fern. So is it safe to eat? Though it has been shown that there is a higher incidence of stomach cancer in those cultures who routinely eat bracken, those who occasionally consume bracken believe that there is little cause for concern.

GOOSEFOOT FAMILY (CHENOPODIACEAE)

These are herb or shrubs, often preferring saline soils. These succulent or scurfy plants are generally considered weeds. The leaves are simple, without stipules, alternately arranged (rarely opposite), and in some cases, reduced to scales. The small flowers, often inconspicuous, have a calyx of 5 or fewer sepals; the calyx is absent in the female flowers. There are usually as many stamens as sepals, but sometimes there are fewer. The ovary is superior, which means that the stamens are connected beneath the ovary. The one-celled ovary develops into a dry, one-seeded indehiscent fruit. There are 1,400 species worldwide.

EXAMPLES

Glasswort, samphire, or pickleweed (*Salicornia* spp.), lamb's quarters (*Chenopodium album*), Russian thistle or tumbleweed (*Salsola* spp.), saltbush (*Atriplex* spp.) including redscale, arrowscale, crownscale, orach, garden or sugar beets (*Beta vulgaris*), sea blite (*Suaeda* spp.), winged pigweed (*Cycloloma atriplicifolium*), etc.

USES

The leaves of many can be eaten raw in salads. Older greens often need cooking to render them less bitter and more palatable. Seeds of most members can be harvested, winnowed, and used as a flour or flour extender.

CAUTIONS

Some species become quite woody and fibrous when mature. Some leaves will cause a severe irritation in the mouth and throat if eaten raw.

GRASS (ALL SPECIES)

There are about 10,000 species of the grasses worldwide (divided into about 600 genera). We find about 1,000 of those species in the United States.

(See the main text under Grass for the description, examples, uses, and cautions.)

MALLOW FAMILY (MALVACEAE)

These are herbs or soft-woody shrubs with mucilaginous juice, tough fibrous inner bark, and covered with small evenly scattered hairs. There are about 1,500 species of the mallow family worldwide, divided into 85 genera. The leaves are alternately arranged, simple, and palmately lobed. The flower has a 5-lobed calyx and 5 petals that are twisted in the bud. There is an indefinite number of stamens, which are joined together in a column or tube around the pistil, attached on the receptacle beneath the ovary. This pistil is composed of several carpels, each of which separates upon maturity.

EXAMPLES

Checker bloom (*Sidalcea malviflora*), desert mallow, globe mallow, or apricot mallow (*Sphaeralcea ambigua*), hollyhock (*Althaea* spp.), mallow or cheeseweed (*Malva* spp.), rose mallow (*Hibiscus* spp.), etc.

USES

The leaves of all of these can be eaten raw in salads or cooked like spinach. The roots of some are tender enough to be used like parsnips. The flowers and fruits are edible raw or cooked.

CAUTIONS

Some parts of some mallows, due to age or the particular species, may be too fibrous to eat.

MINER'S LETTUCE FAMILY (MONTIACEAE)

These are annual or perennial succulent herbs whose entire leaves can be alternately or oppositely arranged, or mostly basal. The flowers are perfect (contain both stamen and pistil). There are normally 2 sepals, up to 9 in one genus. There are commonly from 2 to 19. The flowers open in the sunshine and wither quickly. There are 1 to many stamens. The fruit is a capsule. There are about 230 species worldwide divided into about 22 genera.

EXAMPLES

Bitterroot (*Lewisia rediviva*), desert purslane (*Calandrinia* spp.), miner's lettuce (*Claytonia perfoliata*), pussy-paws (*Calyptridium* spp.), etc.

USES

The entire aboveground plant can usually be eaten raw; it may need to be steamed sometimes for improved palatability. In some cases, roots are used for food. The seeds can also be harvested and eaten.

CAUTIONS

None.

MINT FAMILY (LAMIACEAE)

This family includes mostly aromatic herbs or low-growing shrubs with square stems and leaves that are always simple and opposite. Worldwide, there are about 3,500 species of the mint family. Flowers are formed in dense sessile cymes, which have the appearance of globelike whorls encircling the stem. The sepals are more or less united, frequently 2-lipped, usually 5-lobed. The corolla has a distinct tube and is 2-lipped, commonly with 2 lobes in the upper lip and 3 lobes in the lower lip; or the lips are almost equal and the lobes nearly regular.

EXAMPLES

Horehound (*Marrubium vulgare*), true mints (*Mentha* spp.) such as pepper-mint, spearmint, bergamot mint, pennyroyal, horsemint (*Monarda* spp.), catnip (*Nepeta cataria*), true sages (*Salvia* spp.) such as white sage, thistle sage, chia, black sage, and lavender, etc.

USES

Some of these plants are more aromatic than others. Many of the leaves are used for beverages or medicinal tea, particularly the mints, sages, and horehound. The seeds of many can be harvested and used in bread products, ground into flour, or used in tea. The most notable seed source is chia (*Salvia columbariae*) and other Salvias.

CAUTIONS

Don't use the leaves for tea if the flavor or aroma is unpleasant or disagreeable to you. One member, wooly blue curls (*Trichostema lanatum*), has been used to stun fish in small pools of water. Do not use wooly blue curls for tea.

MUSTARD FAMILY (BRASSICACEAE)

All members of the mustard family are herbs with alternate leaves and flowers in terminal racemes. There are 4 distinct sepals and 4 (usually colorful) petals in a cross or x-form. There are 6 stamens, 4 long and 2 short. There is 1 pistil whose stigma is 2-lobed or 1-lobed. The fruit can be a two-celled silique or one-celled and indehiscent. The fruit (commonly called a "pod" or "capsule") can be long and narrow, short and roundish, or flattened. The herbage typically has the strong, pungent mustard-like juice. Worldwide there are 3,200 species divided into about 375 genera.

EXAMPLES

Bladderpod (*Lesquerella* spp.), broccoli, common mustards (*Brassica* spp.), hedge mustard (*Sisymbrium* spp.), pennycress (*Thlaspi* spp.), peppergrass (*Lepidium* spp.), sea rocket (*Cakile edentula* and *C. marítima*), shepherd's purse (*Capsella bursa-pastoris*), squaw cabbage (*Caulanthus* spp.), sweet alyssum (*Lobularia maritima*), tansy mustard (*Descurainia* spp.), toothwort (*Cardamine* spp.), tur-nip, wallflower (*Erysimum* spp.), watercress (*Nasturtium officinale*), wild radish (*Raphanus sativus*), wintercress (*Barbarea* spp.), etc.

USES

Mustard leaves add a spicy flavor to salads and make a good steamed vegetable or spinach-type dish. The flowers, unopened flower buds, and many of the tender fruits can also be added to salads or cooked foods.

CAUTIONS

Older mustard plants tend to be quite bitter, and sometimes spicy hot, so they usually need to be cooked to be palatable. Also, you may encounter tough and woody specimens, which are generally inedible.

OAK FAMILY (ALSO CALLED BEECH FAMILY) (FAGACEAE)

The oak family includes oak trees, beeches, chestnuts, and chinquapins. By some counts, there are about 900 species worldwide. Even children readily recognize oaks by their fruit—the acorn—with its scaly cap. Most members are trees, some are shrubs, and most have deciduous leaves.

(See "Oak Tree" in the main text for a more detailed description.)

EXAMPLES

Beechnuts, black oak, bur oak, chestnuts, live oak, scrub oak, spiny chinquapin, etc.

USES

The nuts (such as acorns) are eaten. (See the main text for the processing of acorns.) In some cases, the bark and leaves may be used for medicinal and craft purposes.

CAUTIONS

Though the acorns are a good food, you must leach out the bitter tannic acid before you use them.

(See the main text for directions.)

ONIONS (*ALLIUM* SPP.)

True onions belong to the onion or garlic family (Alliaceae) (formerly a part of the lily family, Liliaceae). They are perennial herbs, with a leafless flower stalk arising from a bulb, and in some cases, a corm. All the basal leaves are grasslike, with a most typical oniony aroma when crushed. The petals and sepals (perianth segments) are indistinguishable from each other in appearance. Yet they are distinct from each other—they are not fused or united into a basal tube. There are 6 perianth segments: 3 sepals and 3 petals, all the same color. There are 6 stamens and 1 pistil per flower, and the seeds are black, flat, and wrinkled, with one or two seeds per cell.

EXAMPLES

Chives, garlic, leek, shallot, swamp onion, etc.

USES

Some Native American tribes subsisted almost entirely on onions during certain parts of the year. Onions are great added raw to salads, made into soup, or used as a flavoring for omelettes, vegetable dishes, fish, and meat. Use both the bulbs and the tender shoots.

CAUTIONS

Some members of the lily family are deadly poisonous if eaten. You must check for 3 sepals and 3 petals as well as the distinct onion aroma. There are some true onions that lack the onion aroma. Don't eat any nonaromatic species unless you have absolutely identified them as safe.

In *Know Your Poisonous Plants*, Wilma Roberts James states that wild onions are toxic when eaten in great quantities. However, she neither defined the toxic element nor the amount that constituted "great quantities." Consumed in moderation, wild onions have been used as food for centuries.

PURSLANE FAMILY (PORTULACACEAE)

This family only consists of the Portulaca genus, whose most notable member is the purslane with the fleshy leaves and red, round stems. Until recently, the purslane family also consisted of all the plants that are now classified as miner's lettuce family (Montiaceae). When botanists consider such matters as which plants belong to which family, there are "splitters" and there are "joiners." In this case, the splitters prevailed.

EXAMPLES

Purslane (*Portulaca oleracea*).

USES

The entire aboveground plant can be eaten raw, steamed, boiled, stir-fried, etc. The seeds can also be harvested and eaten.

CAUTIONS

None.

ROSE FAMILY (ROSACEAE)

The rose family consists of herbs, shrubs, and trees, all with alternate leaves. The calyx is 4- or 5-lobed. There are 5 petals (although cultivated rose flowers contain many more petals). There can be 10 or numerous stamens; there is 1 to many simple pistils. Fruits are variable, ranging from a pod (follicle), an achene, a drupe (such as a plum), a cluster of drupelets (such as a blackberry), or a pome (such as an apple). Worldwide there are about 3,000 species divided into 100 genera.

EXAMPLES

Apples, blackberries and raspberries, cinquefoil (*Potentilla* spp.), Cotoneaster, pears, serviceberry (*Amelanchier* spp.), stone fruits (*Prunus* spp.) including peach, cherry, apricot, almond, plum, all wild and cultivated roses (*Rosa* spp.), strawberry (*Fragaria* spp.), toyon (*Heteromeles arbutifolia*), etc.

USES

Many leaves of this group can be eaten, some raw, some when cooked, and some leaves are used for medicinal teas. However, the only valid general statement that can be made about this group is that the petals can be eaten as well as the fruits, if fleshy and palatable. This group contains most of the commonly recognized berries, the bulk of cultivated fruits, all roses, and many wild plants. This is certainly a worthwhile group of plants to know.

CAUTIONS

The leaves of some members of this group contain cyanide. An indicator of this is the bitter-almond aroma that emanates when the leaves are crushed. Do not make tea from such leaves, since a mild cyanide poisoning can result. Also, the seeds of many of the fruits (such as apple, cherry, and apricot) contain cyanide. There is rarely a problem consuming these seeds (or nuts) in small to moderate amounts, but poisonings have occurred when eaten in larger amounts.

SEAWEEDS (GREEN, RED, AND BROWN MARINE ALGAE)

(See "Seaweeds" in the main text for the description, examples, uses, and cautions.)

WALNUTS (JUGLANDACEAE)

Worldwide there are about 60 species in this family, most of which are walnuts. These are deciduous trees with pinnately compound leaves. The male flowers are catkins. The fruit is a 2-lobed, hard-shelled nut enclosed in a sheath.

EXAMPLES

Bitternut, black walnut, butternut, English walnut, hickory nut, pecan, etc.

USES

The nuts of all can be eaten, though in many cases a rock or hammer is required to break the thick, hard shell. The husks of the walnuts and some of the others are used as a black dye.

CAUTIONS

Only eat mature nuts. Also, when collecting the freshly fallen walnuts, the husks can stain hands and clothing, so wear gloves.

USEFUL REFERENCES

Angier, Bradford. *Free for the Eating*. Mechanicsburg, PA: Stackpole Books, 1996.

Baldwin, Bruce G., et al., eds. *The Jepson Manual: Vascular Plants of California*. 2nd ed. Berkeley: University of California Press, 2012. This is the book botanists of California use, and nearly every plant found in Oregon can also be found in California.

Benoliel, Doug. *Northwest Foraging: The Classic Guide to Edible Plants of the Northwest*. Seattle: Skipstone Books, 2011. Benoliel covers more than 50 plants in this guide to Northwest edibles, which includes line drawings and a section on poisonous plants. No marginal foods included.

Campbell, Paul Douglas. *Survival Skills of Native California*. Salt Lake City, UT: Gibbs Smith, 1999. A treasure trove of information about how people in California actually did things, and a large section on plant uses.

Elpel, Tom. *Botany in a Day: The Patterns Method of Plant Identification*. Pony, MT: HOPS Press, 2000. Highly recommended. This is the way that botany should be taught.

Enari, Dr. Leonid. *Plants of the Pacific Northwest*. Portland, OR: Binfords and Mort, 1956. Written by Dr. Enari after he moved to Portland from Estonia, this book covers 663 weeds, wildflowers, shrubs, and trees that are common in the Northwest. Includes 185 line drawings, which means that most plants are not illustrated.

Garcia, Cecilia, and Dr. James Adams. *Healing with Medicinal Plants of the West: Cultural and Scientific Basis for Their Use*. La Crescenta, CA: Abedus Press, 2005. An excellent summary of the common edible and medicinal plants found in Oregon.

Gibbons, Euell. *Stalking the Blue-Eyed Scallop*. New York: David McKay Company, 1964. A good description of many of the foods found on the Pacific coast.

Hitchcock, C. Leo, and Arthur Cronquist. *Flora of the Pacific Northwest*. Seattle: University of Washington Press, 1981. This is the book the botanists of Oregon use. As a book of flora goes, it's designed as a key so you can (hopefully) identify the plant you've found. Mostly botanical text, and technical line drawings throughout. Also has a good glossary (you'll need it).

Kallas, John. *Edible Weeds: Wild Foods from Dirt to Plate*. Salt Lake City, UT: Gibbs Smith, 2010. Though this book covers only fifteen wild foods, they are some of the most common wild foods not only in Oregon but throughout the United States. The full-color book tells you everything from identifying the plant to using it in a variety of recipes. Kallas also teaches classes and is the go-to guy for Oregon and the Pacific Northwest when it comes to wild foods! Reach John Kallas, director of Wild Food Adventures, at Institute for the Study of Edible Wild Plants and Other Foragables, 4125 N. Colonial Ave., Portland, OR 97217-3338; (503) 775-3828; www.wildfoodadventures.com.

JOHN KALLAS

Kirk, Donald. *Wild Edible Plants of Western North America*. Happy Camp, CA: Naturegraph, 1970. Though you generally cannot positively identify plants with this book, it does contain a large number of edible and useful plant descriptions, along with drawings that leave a lot to the imagination. Get this book, and use another book to positively identify the plants.

Moerman, Daniel E. *Native American Ethnobotany*. Portland, OR: Timber Press, 1998. Nearly a thousand pages of descriptions of how every plant known to be used by Native Americans was utilized. No pictures at all, but an incredible resource all in one book.

Taylor, Ronald J. *Northwest Weeds: The Ugly and Beautiful Villains of Fields, Gardens, and Roadsides*. Missoula, MT: Mountain Press Publishing, 1990. An excellent full-color summary of some of the common plants of the Northwest, organized by families.

INDEX

A

A. lappa, 44
Adoxaceae, 30
Alliaceae, 206
Allium spp., 206
Amaranth Family, 34
Amaranth, 34
Amaranthaceae, 34
Amaranthus spp., 34
Amelanchier alnifolia, 179
American Bistort, 165
Apiaceae, 37
Arbutus menziesii, 116
Arctium minus, 44
Arctostaphylos spp., 120
Asparagaceae, 213
Asparagus Family, 213
Asparagus officinalis, 213
Asteraceae, 44
Atriplex hastata, 107

B

B. verna, 74
Barbarea vulgaris, 74
Barberry Family, 67
Berberidaceae, 67
Betulaceae, 70
Birch Family, 70
Bistorta bistortoides, 165
Bittercress, 84
Black Nightshade, 196
Blackberry, 192
Blueberry, 126
Borage (or Waterleaf) Family, 72
Boraginaceae, 72
Bracken Family, 19
Bracken, 19

Brassica spp., 77
Brassicaceae, 74
Bread sources, wild, 239
Broad-Leafed Dock, 172
Brown Algae, 15
Buckwheat Family, 165
Burdock, 44

C

C. maritima, 81
C. murale, 110
Cactaceae, 99
Cactus Family, 99
Cakile edentula, 81
Capsella bursa-pastoris, 86
Cardamine spp., 84
Carrot (or Parsley) Family, 37
Caryophyllaceae, 103
Cat's Ear, 54
Cattail Family, 224
Cattail, 224
Chamerion angustifolium, 152
Chenopodiaceae, 107
Chenopodium album, 110
Chickweed, 103
Chicory, 51
Chlorophyta, 15
Cichorium intybus, 51
Cirsium spp., 47
Claytonia lanceolata, 147
Claytonia perfoliata, 149
Corylus cornuta, 70
Cow Parsnip, 42
Curly Dock, 172
Currants, 137

D

Dandelion, 64
Daucus carota, 37
Dennstaedtiacea, 19

E

Easy-to-recognize wild foods, 237
Elderberry, 29
Ericaceae, 116
Erodium spp., 134
Eudicots, 29
Evening Primrose Family, 152

F

Fagaceae, 130
Fennel, 40
Ferns, 18
Filaree, 134
Fireweed, 152
Foeniculum vulgare, 40
Fragaria spp., 181

G

Gaultheria shallon, 123
Geraniaceae, 134
Geranium Family, 134
Glasswort, 113
Gooseberries, 137
Gooseberry Family, 137
Goosefoot Family, 107
Grass Family, 221
Grossulariaceae, 137
Gymnosperms, 22

H

H. lanatum, 42
Hazelnut, 70
Heath Family, 116
Hedge Mustard, 96
Heracleum maximum, 42
Huckleberry, 126

Hypochaeris radicata, 54

I

Indian Plum, 184

J

Juncaceae, 209
Juncus textilis, 209
Juneberry, 179

L

Lactuca serriola, 56
Lamb's Quarter (Green), 110
Lamb's Quarter (White), 110
Lamiaceae, 141
Lapsana communis, 59
Lauraceae, 26
Laurel Family, 26
Lopseed Family, 158

M

M. matricarioides, 49
Madrone, 116
Magnoliids, 25
Mallow Family, 144
Mallow, 144
Malva neglecta, 144
Malvaceae, 144
Manzanita, 120
Marine Green Algae, 15
Matricaria discoidea, 49
Mentha spp., 141
Mertensia ciliata, 72
Mimulus guttatus, 158
Miner's Lettuce Family, 147
Miner's Lettuce, 149
Mint Family, 141
Mint, 141
Monocots, 205
Montiaceae, 147
Mountain Bluebells, 72

Mountain Sorrel, 168
Muskroot Family, 30
Mustard Family, 74
Mustard, 77

N

Nasturtium officinale, 88
Nettle Family, 199
Nightshade Family, 196
Nipplewort, 59
Nutritional data, 12

O

Oak Family, 130
Oak Tree, 130
Oemleria cerasiformis, 184
Onagraceae, 152
Onion (or Garlic) Family, 206
Opuntia spp., 99
Orach, 107
Oregon Grape, 67
Oregon Myrtle, 26
Oxalidaceae, 156
Oxalis Family, 156
Oxalis spp., 156
Oxyria dignya, 168

P

P. lanceolate, 160
Phaeophyta, 15
Phrymaceae, 158
Pickleweed, 113
Pinaceae, 23
Pine Family, 23
Pine, 23
Pineapple Weed, 49
Pink Family, 103
Pinus spp., 23
Plantaginaceae, 160
Plantago major, 160
Plantain Family, 160

Plantain, 160
Poaceae, 221
Polygonaceae, 165
Portulaca oleracea, 176
Portulacaceae, 176
Prickly Lettuce, 56
Prickly Pear, 99
Prunus spp., 187
Pteridium aquilinum, 19
Purslane Family, 176
Purslane, 176

Q

Quercus spp., 130

R

R. raphanistrum, 92
Raphanus sativus, 92
Red Algae, 15
Rhodophyta, 15
Ribes spp., 137
Rosa spp., 190
Rosaceae, 179
Rose Family, 179
Rubus spp., 192
Rumex acetosella, 170
Rumex crispus, 172
Rumex obtusifolius, 172
Rush Family, 209
Rush, 209

S

Salal, 123
Salicornia spp., 113
Sambucus spp., 30
Sea Rocket, 81
Seaweeds, 14
Serviceberry, 179
Sheep Sorrel, 170
Shepherd's Purse, 86
Sisymbrium spp., 96

Solanaceae, 196
Solanum nigrum, 196
Sonchus oleraceus, 61
Sour Grass, 156
Sow Thistle, 61
Speedwell, 163
Spring Beauty, 147
Stellaria media, 103
Stinging Nettle, 199
Strawberry, 181
Sunflower Family, 44

T

Taraxacum officinale, 64
Thistle, 47
Typha spp., 224
Typhaceae, 224

U

Umbellularia californica, 26
Urtica dioica, 199
Urticaceae, 199

V

Vaccinium spp., 126
Veronica americana, 163
Veronica, 163
Violaceae, 203
Violet Family, 203
Violet, 203

W

Watercress, 88
Wild Asparagus, 213
Wild Carrot, 37
Wild Cherries, 187
Wild Onions, 206
Wild Radish, 92
Wild Rose, 190
Wintercress, 74
Wood Sorrel, 156

Y

Yellow Monkey Flower, 158

ABOUT THE AUTHOR

Christopher Nyerges, cofounder of the School of Self-Reliance, has led wild-food walks for thousands of students since 1974. He has authored twenty-two books, mostly on wild foods, survival, and self-reliance, and thousands of newspaper and magazine articles. He continues to teach where he lives in Los Angeles County, California. More information about his classes and seminars is available at www.schoolofself-reliance.com or by writing to: School of Self-Reliance, Box 41834, Eagle Rock, CA 90041.

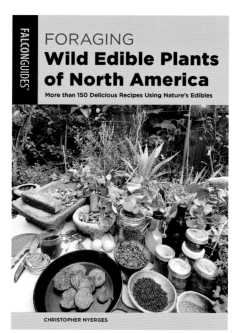

Foraging Wild Edible Plants of North America:
More than 150 Delicious Recipes Using Nature's
Edibles, Second Edition 9781493064472

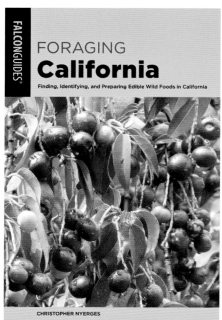

Foraging California: Finding, Identifying, And
Preparing Edible Wild Foods In California, 2nd
Edition 9781493040896

Foraging Washington: Finding, Identifying, and
Preparing Edible Wild Foods 9781493025336

Foraging Idaho: Finding, Identifying, and Preparing
Edible Wild Foods 9781493031900